# Mihuma

-----

### Anecdotes to bridge the generation gap

### A light-hearted approach

To Mrs Allan,

Sorry to hear you had to rush back for Florida

Wishing you a speedy recovery -

So you can go travelling again. + See page 36 !

Warm regards

Sabine & Jeremy

Richard Smouha was born in 1932. Educated at Harrow School and Magdalene College, Cambridge, he took a degree in Economics and Law after two years National Service in the RAF. He was called to the Bar in 1959 and then obtained a degree in French law from Paris University.

After serving as a company lawyer in Geneva, he was employed in Swiss banking before setting up as an independent investment adviser and bond fund manager.

He and his wife Sylvia have three children, each of whom has three children.

# Dedication

Dedicated to my father who started this collection
and my mother who continued it.

# Thanks to

Brian Levin for editing the text and helping
with the self-publishing process,
Bob Naggar for his help on the computer
and Serge Kaplun for his professional encouragement.

# TABLE OF CONTENTS

# INTRODUCTION

- 
- 

The main object of this book is to show the major differences happening in the world and the speed at which they are being accepted, creating a major generation gap between today's elders and the next two generations. I have attempted to do this over a widespread number of facets of life and in each case provide examples, inevitably amusing.

This is not a book to be read from cover to cover. It will be found most useful in doctor's or dentist's waiting rooms, in train stations or at airports, but not on planes. It should not be left around. I personally think it is best to read it for only ten or fifteen minutes at a time.

It is a book to be visited, but unlike most visits it can at any time be temporarily abandoned. You, the visitor, are in charge, deciding how often and how long you visit.

I have tried to facilitate visiting by putting the items into categories, but this may defeat its own object where an item could be equally appropriate in two or three other places.

Another question I faced was, what is fact and what is fiction? This is not as easy as it sounds because of the way the internet is becoming increasingly used in our new world. Many readers (indeed often rightly) believe that "fact is stranger than fiction," and so the borderline between the two has become more and more obscure.

You will doubtless come across items with which you already familiar, but I trust this will not spoil your enjoyment, for there is also a wealth of personal, unpublished (even on the net) and ancient items that I hope will make purchase of this little tome worthwhile.

All reactions, appreciation or criticisms, are welcome.


Conches, 1 December 2013

---

## TWO STORIES FROM CHICAGO

### Easy Eddie

Many years ago, Al Capone virtually owned Chicago. Capone was not famous for anything heroic. He was notorious for involving the "windy" city in everything from bootlegged booze and prostitution to murder.

Capone had a lawyer nicknamed Easy Eddie. He was Capone's lawyer for a good reason: he was very good! In fact Eddie's skill at legal manoeuvring was so good that he kept Big Al out of jail for a long time.

To show his appreciation, Capone paid him very well. Not only was the money big, but Eddie got special dividends as well. For instance he and his family occupied a fenced-in mansion with live-in help and all the conveniences of the day. The estate was so large that it filled an entire Chicago city block.

Eddie lived the high life of the Chicago mob and gave little consideration to the atrocities that went on around him. He did have one soft spot however. He had a son whom he loved dearly. Eddie saw to it that his young son had clothes, cars and a good education. Nothing was withheld. Price was no object. And despite his involvement with organised crime, Eddie tried to teach him right from wrong. Eddie wanted his son to be a better man than he was. Yet with all his wealth and influence, there were two things he couldn't give his son: a good name and a good example.

One day Eddie reached a difficult decision. Easy Eddie wanted to rectify the wrongs he had done. He decided he would go to the authorities and tell the truth about Al "Scarface" Capone, clean up his tarnished name and offer his son some semblance of integrity. To do this, he would have to testify against The Mob, and he knew that the cost would be great.

So, he testified. Within the year, Easy Eddie's life ended in a blaze of gunfire on a lonely Chicago street. But in his eyes he had given his son the greatest gift he had to offer, at the greatest price he could ever pay. Police removed from his pockets, a rosary, a crucifix, a religious medallion and the following poem clipped from a magazine:

*The clock of life is wound but once.*
*And no man has the power*
*To tell just when the hands will stop,*
*At late or early hour.*

*To lose one's wealth is sad indeed.*
*To lose one's health is more.*
*To lose one's soul is such a loss,*
*That no man can restore*

*Today only is our own.*
*So live, love, and toil with a will.*
*Place no faith in tomorrow,*
*For the clock may soon be still.*

(Author: Robert H. Smith)

## Butch O'Hare

World War 2 produced many heroes. One such man was Lieutenant Commander Butch O'Hare. He was a fighter pilot assigned to the aircraft carrier Lexington in the South Pacific. One day his entire squadron was sent on a mission. After he was airborne, he looked at his fuel gauge and realised that someone had forgotten to top off his fuel tank. He would not have enough fuel to complete his mission and get back to his ship. His flight leader told him to return to the Carrier. Reluctantly he dropped out of formation and headed back to the fleet.

As he was returning to the mother ship, he saw something that turned his blood cold: a squadron of Japanese aircraft was speeding its way to the American fleet.

The American fighters were gone on a sortie and the fleet was all but defenceless. He was unable to reach his squadron and bring them back in time to save the fleet. Nor was he able to warn the fleet of the approaching danger. There was only one thing to do. He had to divert the enemy somehow from reaching the fleet. Laying aside all thoughts of personal safety, he dived into the formation of Japanese planes. Wing-mounted 50-calibres blazed as he charged in, attacking one surprised enemy plane, and then another. Butch wove in and out of the now broken formation and fired at as many planes as possible until all his ammunition was finally spent. Undaunted he continued the assault trying to clip a wing or a tail in the hope of damaging as many planes as possible, rendering them unfit to fly. Finally the Japanese squadron, in exasperation, took off in another direction.

Deeply relieved, Butch O'Hare and his battered fighter limped back to the Carrier. Upon arrival, he reported in and related the event surrounding his return. The film from the gun-carrier mounted on his plane told the tale. It showed the extent of Butch's daring attempt to protect his fleet. He had in fact destroyed five enemy aircraft.

This took place on 20th February 1942, and for that action Butch became the US Navy's first Ace of World War Two and the first naval aviator to win the Congressional Medal of Honor.

A year later, Butch was killed in aerial combat at the age of 29. His home town would not allow the memory of this WW2 hero to fade, and today, O'Hare airport in Chicago is named in tribute to the courage of this great man. So O'Hare airport has honoured Butch by creating a memorial in his name which can be found between Terminals 1 and 2 and which displays his statue and his Medal of Honor.

The surprising and touching connection between these two spectacular but sad stories:

### *BUTCH O'HARE WAS EASY EDDIE'S SON !*

*An Associated Press true story, reported by Kurt Westervelt*

At the 1994 annual awards dinner given for Forensic Science, AAFS President Dr. Don Harper Mills astounded his audience with the legal complications of a bizarre death.

On 23rd March 1994, the medical examiner viewed the body of Ronald Opus and concluded that he had died from a shotgun wound to the head. Mr. Opus had jumped from the top of a ten story building intending to commit suicide. He left a note indicating his despondency.

As he fell past the ninth floor, his life was interrupted by a shotgun blast passing through a window and which killed him instantly. Neither the shooter nor the deceased was aware that a safety net had been installed just below the eighth floor level to protect some building workers and that Ronald Opus would not have been able to complete his suicide the way he had planned.

Ordinarily, according to Dr. Mills, someone who sets out to commit suicide and ultimately succeeds even though the mechanism may not have been what he intended, is still defined as committing suicide. That Mr. Opus was shot on the way to certain death, but probably would not have been successful because of the safety net, caused the medical examiner to feel that he had a homicide on his hands.

The room on the ninth floor from where the shotgun blast emanated was occupied by an elderly man and his wife. They were arguing vigorously and he was threatening her with a shotgun. The man was so upset that when he pulled the trigger, he completely missed his wife and the pellets went through the window, striking Mr. Opus.

When one intends to kill subject A but kills subject B in the attempt one is guilty of the murder of subject B. When inevitably confronted with the murder charge, the old man and his wife were both adamant and both said that they thought the gun was not loaded. The old man said that it was a long-standing habit to threaten his wife with the unloaded shotgun. He had had no intention to murder her. Therefore the killing of Mr. Opus appeared to be an accident, that is, assuming that the gun had been accidentally loaded.

The continuing investigation turned up a witness who saw the old couple's son loading the shotgun about six weeks prior to the fatal accident.

It transpired that the old lady had cut off her son's financial support and that the son, knowing the propensity of his father to use the shotgun threateningly, loaded the gun with the expectation that his father would shoot his mother.

Since the loader of the gun was aware of this, he was guilty of murder even though he did not actually pull the trigger. The case now becomes one of murder on the part of the son for the death of Ronald Opus.

Further investigation revealed that the son was in fact Ronald Opus. He had become increasingly despondent over the failure of his attempt to engineer his mother's murder. This led him to jump off the ten story building on 23rd March only to be killed by a shotgun blast passing through the ninth floor window. The son had actually murdered himself, so the medical examiner closed the case as a suicide.

*This case fascinates me, as I believe one could more easily argue in favour of either accidental death or manslaughter, depending on the weighting of intent, which in my view is more important than the bare facts in this case. Personally I would have argued against suicide as it was really an unsuccessful attempt at suicide and more in favour of either homicide or accidental death.*

### How to treat a rude customer

A crowded Malta-London flight leaving from Luqua airport was cancelled at the last minute. Unexpectedly, the gate attendant found herself alone and in charge of re-booking a long line of inconvenienced travellers. Suddenly an angry passenger pushed his way to the desk, in front of the line. He slapped his ticket down on the counter and proclaimed, "I HAVE to be on this flight and it HAS to be FIRST CLASS."

The attendant replied, "I'm sorry Sir, I'll be happy to try to help you, but I've got to help these people first, and I'm sure we'll be able to work something out."

The passenger was unimpressed. He asked loudly so that all the passengers behind him could hear, "DO YOU HAVE ANY IDEA WHO I AM?"

Without hesitating the attendant smiled and grabbed her public address microphone: "May I have your attention please? May I have your attention please?" she began. With her voice being clearly heard throughout the terminal, she announced, "We have a passenger here at Gate 14 WHO DOES NOT KNOW WHO HE IS. If anyone can help him find his identity, please come to Gate 14."

With the passengers behind him in the queue laughing hysterically, the man glared at the attendant, gritted his teeth and said, "F*** you!"

Without flinching, she smiled and replied, "I'm sorry, Sir but you'll have to get in the queue for that too."

dear Captain
My name is Nicola im 8
years. old, this is my first
flight but im not scared. I
like to watch the clouds go
by. My mum says the crew is
nice. I think your plane is
good. thanks for a nice flight
dont f... up the landing
LuV Nicola
Xx x x

*Actual drawing (dots added) handed to a
flight attendant on a Quantas flight
by an 8-year-old girl*

## How hot is Hell?

*The following story told by a Professor at Yale University is claimed to be true*

A thermodynamics professor had written a take-home exam for his graduate students. It had just one question: *"Is Hell exothermic (gives off heat) or endothermic (absorbs heat)? Support your answer with a proof."*
Most of the students wrote proofs of their beliefs using Boyle's Law (gas cools off when it expands and heats up when it is compressed). One student however wrote the following:
First we need to know how the mass of Hell is changing over time. So, we need to know the rate that souls are moving into Hell and the rate they are leaving. We can assume that once a soul gets to Hell, it will not leave.
As for how many souls are entering Hell, let's look at the different religions that exist in the world today. Some of these religions state that if you are not a member of their religion you will go to Hell. Since there are more than one of these religions, and since most people do not belong to more than one religion, we can assume that all souls will go to Hell. With birth and death rates as they are, we can expect the number of souls in Hell to increase exponentially.
Next, Boyle's Law states that in order for the temperature and pressure in Hell to stay the same, the volume of Hell has to expand as souls are added.
This gives two possibilities: If Hell expands at a lower rate than the rate at which souls enter, then the pressure and temperature in Hell will increase until all Hell breaks loose.
Of course, if Hell expands at a rate faster than the increase of souls in Hell, then the temperature and pressure will drop until Hell freezes over.

If we accept the postulate given to me by Miss Therese Banyan during my freshman year that, "It will be a cold night in Hell before I sleep with you," and take into account the fact that I still have not succeeded with her, then point 2 cannot be true.;

Therefore, Hell is exothermic.

This student got the only A of the class.

*Daily Mail, Tuesday 19 March 2013*

## MAN WITH NO SHAME: "I MUST TRAVEL FIRST CLASS"

The much criticised head of the NHS Insisted yesterday that he had to travel first class in order to do his job effectively.
The £48,900 of travel expenses he had notched up (the equivalent cost of employing two nurses for a year) included 41 trips to Birmingham, where his new 35 year old wife lives with their baby daughter.

## Move over!

*The following is an actual radio conversation that took place in thick fog at sea on 10th October 1995 and whose release was authorised by the Chief of Naval Operations.*

Party 1 – Please divert your course 15 degrees to the North to avoid a collision.
Party 2 – Recommend you divert YOUR course 15 degrees to the South to avoid a collision.
Party 1 – This is the Captain of a US Navy Ship. I say again, divert your course.
Party 2 – No. I say again, you divert YOUR course!
Party 1 – THIS IS THE AIRCRAFT CARRIER ENTERPRISE. WE ARE A LARGE WARSHIP OF THE US NAVY. DIVERT YOUR COURSE NOW!
Party 2 – This is a lighthouse. Your call!

### It'll never be the same again

A grandson asked his grandmother what she thought about the shootings at schools, the computer age, and just things in general.

The grandmother replied, "Well, let me think a minute. I was born before television, penicillin, polio shots, frozen foods, Xerox, contact lenses, frisbees, the pill. There were no credit cards, laser beams, ballpoint pens. Man had not yet invented pantyhose, air conditioners, dishwashers, clothes-dryers. The clothes were hung out to dry in the fresh air and man hadn't yet walked on the moon.

"Your Grandfather and I got married first, and then lived together. Every family had a father and a mother. Until I was 25, I called every man older than me 'Sir'. And after I turned 25, I still called policemen and every man with the title 'Sir'.

"We were before gay rights, dual careers, daycare centres, computer-dating and group therapy. Our lives were governed by the Ten Commandments, good judgement and common sense. We were taught to know the difference between right and wrong and to stand up and take responsibility for our actions. Serving your country was a privilege; living in this country was a bigger privilege.

"We thought that fast food was what you ate at Lent. Having a meaningful relationship was getting along with your cousins. Draft dodgers were those who closed front doors when the evening breeze started. Time-sharing meant time the family spent time together in the evenings and at weekends, not purchasing condominiums.

"We had never heard of FM radios, tape decks, CDs, electric typewriters, yogurt or guys wearing earrings

"We listened to big bands, Jack Benny, and the President's speeches on our radios. And I don't remember any kid blowing his brains out listening to Tommy Dorsey. "If you saw anything with 'Made in Japan' on it, it was junk.
"The term 'making out' referred to how you did in your school exam.
"Pizza Hut, McDonalds and instant coffee were unheard of.

"We had 5-10 cent stores where you could actually buy things for 5-10 cents. Ice-cream cones, phone calls (sometimes through an operator), rides on a streetcar, and a Pepsi were all 10 cents. You could buy a new Ford Coupe for $600 with gas at 11 cents a gallon.
"In my day, 'grass' was mowed, 'coke' was a cold drink, 'pot' was something your mother cooked in, 'rock music' was your grandmother's lullaby, 'AIDS' were helpers in the Principal's office, 'chip' meant a piece of wood, 'hardware' was found in a hardware store, and 'software' wasn't even a word.
"We were the last generation to actually believe that a lady needed a husband to have a baby.
"No wonder there is a generation gap! After all, I am only 59 years old, born in 1952."

## *Punctuality*

Charlie, a big active man in his sixties, needed something to do after retirement. He found a job as a retiree-greeter at the local largish Walmart department store. His function was to stand at the entrance and direct people to wherever or whatever they wanted to do. He had a great personality and regulars would stop to chat with him. But there was a small problem --- Charlie just couldn't get to work on time, was consistently ten to twenty minutes late for his shift. But he was a good worker, really tidy, clean-shaven, sharp-minded and a real credit to the company, demonstrating their "Older Person Friendly" policies. One day, the boss called him into the office for a talk. "Charley, I have to tell you, I like your work ethic, you do a bang-up job when you finally get here; but your being late so often is quite bothersome. You're a really nice guy, everyone likes you and you're a great PR for the store. But we do have a small problem with your punctuality on the shift."

"I know, Boss, and I'm working on it."

"That's fine, Charlie, you're a team player. That's what I like to hear."

"Yes sir, I understand your concern and I'll try harder."

Then he paused a moment and seeming puzzled went on to comment, "You know, Charley, I was looking at your file and saw that you spent the whole of your career in the Armed Forces, and I just wondered what did they say when you turned up so late and so often?"

The old man looked down at the floor, then looked up, gave a big smile and said with a grin: "They usually saluted and said, 'Good morning, Admiral, can I get you your coffee, Sir?'"

## Soap opera

*The following is correspondence between a London hotel's staff and one of its guests. The London hotel submitted it to the Sunday Times on a no-name basis. I will call the guest Brian McLean.*

Dear Maid,

Please do not leave any more of those little bars of soap in my bathroom as I have brought with me my own bath-sized Dial soap. Please remove the six unopened little bars from the shelf under the medicine chest as well as the three in the shower soap dish. They are in my way.

Thank you.

*B. McLean*

Dear Room 635,

I am not your regular maid. She will be back tomorrow, Thursday, from her day off. I took the three hotel soaps out of the shower soap dish as you requested. The six bars on your shelf I took out of your way and put on top of your Kleenex dispenser in case you should change your mind. This leaves only the three bars I left today since my instructions from the management are to leave 3 soaps daily. I hope this is satisfactory.

*Kathy, relief maid*

Dear Maid,

I hope you are my regular maid. Apparently Kathy did not tell you about my note to her concerning the little bars of soap. When I got back to my room this evening I found that you had added 3 little Camays to the shelf under my medicine cabinet. I am going to be here in the hotel for two weeks and have brought my own bath-size Dial soap so I won't need these 6 little Camays on the shelf. They are in my way when shaving, brushing teeth, etc. Please remove them.

*B. McLean*

Dear Mr. McLean,

My day off was last Wed. So the relief maid left 3 hotel soaps as instructed by the management. I took the 6 soaps which were in your way on the shelf and put them in the soap dish where your Dial was. I put the Dial in the medicine cabinet for your convenience.
I didn't remove the three complimentary soaps which are always placed inside the medicine cabinet for all new check-ins and which you did not object to when you checked in last Monday. Please let me know if I can be of further assistance.

*Your regular maid, Dotty*

Dear Mr. McLean,

The assistant manager, Mr. Kensedder, informed me this morning that you called him last evening and said you were unhappy with your maid service. I have assigned a new girl to your room. I hope you will accept my apologies for any past inconvenience. If you have any future complaints please contact me so that I can give it my personal attention. Call extension 1108 between 8 am and 5 pm. Thank you.

*Elaine Carmen, Housekeeper*

Dear Miss Carmen,

It is impossible to contact you by phone since I leave the hotel for business at 7.45 am and only get back between 5.30 and 6 pm. That is the reason I called Mr. Kensedder last night. You were already off duty. I only asked Mr. Kensedder if he could do anything about those little bars of soap. The new maid that you assigned to me must have thought I was a new check-in today, since she left another 3 bars of soap in my medicine cabinet along with her regular delivery of 3 bars on the bathroom shelf. In just 5 days I have accumulated 24 little bars of soap. Why are you doing this to me?

*B. McLean*

Dear Mr. McLean,

Your maid, Kathy, has been instructed to stop delivering soap to your room and remove the extra soaps. If I can be of further assistance please call 1108 between 8 am and 5 pm. Thank you.

*Elaine Carmen, Housekeeper*

Dear Mr. Kensedder,

My bath-size Dial is missing. Every bar of soap was taken from my room including MY own bath-size Dial. I came in last night and had to call the bellhop to bring me 4 little Cashmere Bouquets.

*B. McLean*

Dear Mr. McLean,

I have informed our housekeeper Elaine Carmen of your problem. I cannot understand why there was no soap in your room as our maids are instructed to leave 3 bars of soap each time they service a room. The situation will be rectified immediately. Please accept my apologies for the inconvenience.

*Martin I. Kensedder, Assistant Manager*

Dear Mrs. Carmen,

Who the hell left 54 little bars of soap of Camay in my room? I came in last night and found 54 little bars of soap. I don't want 54 little bars of Camay. I want my one damn bar of bath-size Dial. Do you realize I have 54 bars of soap in here? All I want is my bath-size Dial. Please give me back my bath-size Dial.

*B. McLean*

Dear Mr. McLean,

You complained of too much soap in your room so I had them removed. Then you complained to Mr. Kensedder that all your soap was missing so I personally returned them. The 24 Camays which had been taken and the 3 Camays you are supposed to receive daily. I don't know anything about the 4 Cashmere Bouquets. Obviously your maid, Kathy, did not know I had returned your soap so she also brought 24 Camays plus the 3 daily Camays. I don't know where you got the idea that this hotel provides bath-size Dial. I was able to locate some Bath-size Ivory which I left in your room.

*Elaine Carmen, Housekeeper*

Dear Mrs. Carmen,

Just a short note to bring you up to date on my soap inventory. As of today I possess: On shelf under medicine cabinet – 18 Camay in 4 stacks of 4 and 1 stack of 2. On Kleenex dispenser – 11 Camay in 2 stacks of 4 and 1 stack of 3. On bedroom dresser – 1 stack of Cashmere Bouquet, 1 stack of hotel-size Ivory - and 8 Camay in 2 stacks of 4. Inside medicine cabinet – 14 Camay in 3 stacks of 4 and 1 stack of 3. In shower soap dish – 6 Camay, very moist. On northeast corner of tub 1 Cashmere Bouquet slightly used. On northwest corner of tub – 6 Camays in 2 stacks of 3.

Please ask Kathy, when she services my room, to make sure the stacks are neatly piled and dusted. Also, please advise her that the stacks of more than 4 have a tendency to tip. May I suggest that my bedroom window-sill is not in use and will make an excellent spot for future soap deliveries? One more item: I have purchased another bar of bath-sized Dial which I am keeping in the hotel vault to avoid further misunderstandings.

*B. McLean*

*A report by AFP dating from the mid-fifties and which I copied from the newspaper:*

## WIFE THROWN OUT

A man threw his wife from a window of their second floor flat in Cairo because his dinner was not ready. She suffered multiple fractures. He was freed on 8 pounds bail. In his summing up the judge remarked that he was lucky ---- if he had pushed his donkey, which was on the balcony, the bail would have been 15 pounds.

* * * * *

### Each man for himself

*The following story was sent, I believe, to the Daily Telegraph some thirty years ago by a Susan Sampson, living in Hove, East Sussex in England. My mother knowing the story, cut it out and sent it to me.*

The story is that we were on a family ski day in Villars and there was a longish queue for the four-person bubbles to the top of the ski-run. An empty cabin came along and a man thrust his way through our group, completely pushing them aside and jumped into the cabin placing his skis in one of the four outside racks on the cabin.

I stepped forward and said in French, "Excuse me, but we were in front of you." He replied with a chuckle "In life it's each man for himself." By this time the platform supervisor had stepped forward and locked the cabin door.

As soon as this was done and he was properly locked in, I took his skis out of the rack. To this day I smile when I think of his change of expression from proud conquering hero to ski-less tourist as I shouted through the open window of the cabin, "You too have to learn that in life it's each man for himself"

Vérité à ne pas manquer de lire et qu'il avait rai

Et bien, les grands de ce monde nous réserver
surprises sur leurs textes d'il y a 50 ans...

## Citations du Général De Gaulle
1959

rapportées par Alain Peyrefitte

Maintenant, on irait en prison pour bien moins (

« C'est très bien qu'il y ait des Français jaunes, des Français bruns. Ils montrent que la France est ouverte à toutes les races et qu'elle a une vocation universelle. Mais à condition qu'ils restent une petite minorité. Sinon, la France ne serait plus la France. Nous sommes quand même avant tout un peuple européen de race blanche, de culture grecque et latine et de religion chrétienne. Qu'on ne se raconte pas d'histoire ! Les musulmans, vous êtes allés les voir ? Vous les avez regardés avec leurs turbans et leurs djellabas ? Vous voyez bien que ce ne sont pas des Français. Ceux qui prônent l'intégration ont une cervelle de colibri, même s'ils sont très savants. Essayez d'intégrer de l'huile et du vinaigre. Agitez la bouteille. Au bout d'un moment, ils se sépareront de nouveau. Les Arabes sont des Arabes, les Français sont des Français. Vous croyez que le corps français peut absorber dix millions de musulmans, qui demain seront vingt millions et après-demain quarante ? Si nous faisions l'intégration, si tous les Arabes et les Berbères d'Algérie étaient considérés comme Français, comment les empêcherez-vous de venir s'installer en métropole, alors que le niveau de vie y est tellement plus élevé ? Mon village ne s'appellerait plus Colombey-les-Deux-Églises, mais Colombey-les-Deux-Mosquées. »

CHARLES DE GAULLE

**Well, the great of this world surprise us with their texts of 50 years ago ...**
Quote from General De Gaulle
1959
reported by Alain Peyrefitte

Today, one would go to jail for much less

"It is very good that there are yellow French people and brown French people. They show that France is open to all races and that it has a universal culture. But on condition that they remain a small minority. Otherwise, France would not be France. We are still primarily a European people of white race, Greek and Latin culture and Christian religion. Let's not kid ourselves! Muslims, have you been to see them? Have you seen them with their turbans and djellabas? You can clearly see that they are not French. Those who advocate integration have the brain of a hummingbird, even if they are very knowledgeable. Try to mix oil and vinegar. Shake the bottle. After a while, they will separate again. Arabs are Arabs, and French are French. If you believe that the French population can absorb ten million Muslims, who tomorrow will be twenty million and forty the day after tomorrow? If we carried out integration, if all the Arabs and Berbers of Algeria were considered French, how would you prevent them from coming to settle in France, where the standard of living is so much higher? My village would not be called Colombey-les-Deux-Eglises (churches) anymore, but Colombey-les-Deux-Mosques.

CHARLES DE GAULLE

# Drôle d'aventure au cimetière

Vendredi matin 22 mai. Cimetière de Chêne-Bougeries. Une jeune femme dépose deux plantes sur la tombe de son père; mais, ne disposant d'aucun outil, elle n'arrive pas à les enfouir dans la terre. C'est alors qu'un vieil ami de la famille (87 ans) se propose de faire le nécessaire et tentera, l'après-midi, muni d'une truelle, de creuser deux trous. Ne pouvant toutefois faire cela en demeurant debout, il s'agenouillera devant la tombe et c'est sans problème qu'il s'exécutera. Mais, une fois le travail terminé, il tentera de se relever mais n'y arrivera pas.

Après de répétés et vains efforts, il s'agrippera à la croix en bois plantée à la tête de la tombe, qui ne résistera pas. Il s'approchera ensuite d'une tombe voisine ayant une pierre tombale d'environ 50 cm de hauteur. A nouveau, impossible de se remettre sur pied. Qu'importe, il se couchera le long de la tombe en attendant la venue d'un visiteur ou d'un employé du cimetière. Mais personne ne se pointera dans cette nouvelle et encore peu occupée partie du cimetière. Il ne lui restera alors qu'à utiliser son portable pour appeler des amis. Hélas tous absents.

Après une nouvelle attente, toujours couché, il constatera qu'il a de la peine à mouvoir ses pieds. Craignant alors quelque chose de grave, il décidera de téléphoner au 144. Quelques instants plus tard, une ambulance se signalera par son habituel "pimpon". Mais personne n'arrive 10 minutes s'écouleront jusqu'à ce qu'enfin une tête n'apparaisse derrière un muret. Notre homme se signalera et sera vu. L'ambulance pénétrera alors dans le cimetière et deux ambulanciers se précipiteront vers notre homme. Sans peine, ils le remettront sur pied. L'usage d'une civière sera inutile et il

suffira qu'il s'assoie sur un siège de l'ambulance.

– Et maintenant, où devons-nous vous conduire?

– Eh bien chez moi…

– Impossible, Monsieur, c'est soit l'hôpital soit une institution habilitée à vous recevoir.

– Dans ce cas, le service d'urgence de la Clinique des Grangettes, à quelques centaines de mètres.

– OK.

A la clinique, on placera notre vieil homme dans un fauteuil roulant avant qu'un médecin, qui tardera à venir, puisse l'examiner attentivement avant d'envoyer un diagnostic à son médecin traitant.

– Il n'y a pas de problème grave, vous pouvez dès lors rentrer chez vous, Monsieur.

Entretemps, la jeune femme ayant voulu fleurir la tombe de son père pourra être alertée et d'un tragi-comique et accompagnera notre héros jusqu'au… cimetière où il récupérera sa voiture et retournera chez lui.

Conclusion, grand merci à l'assurance maladie CPT!    **IPS**

Publicité

**Translation on opposite page**

## *A strange adventure at the cemetery*

Friday morning, 22 May, at the Chêne-Bougeries Cemetery Geneva. A young woman placed two plants on her father's grave, but having no tools, was unable to plant them in the earth. Then an old friend of the family (aged 87) offered to do what was needed and attempted to dig two holes with a trowel. Unable to do this standing up, he knelt before the grave and carried it out with no problem. But once the work was finished, he tried to get up but could not do so.

After repeated unsuccessful efforts, he took hold of the wooden cross at the head of the grave, but it gave way. Then he approached a nearby tomb, which had a tombstone about 50 cm high. Again, he could not stand up. No matter, he lay down by the grave awaiting the arrival of a visitor or a cemetery employee. But nobody showed up in this new and barely occupied part of the cemetery. His only recourse was to call his friends on his cell phone, alas all absent.

A little later, still lying down, he found he had difficulty moving his feet. Fearing something serious, he decided to call 144, emergency. Soon he heard the siren of an ambulance, but nobody appeared. Ten minutes later a head appeared above a low wall. Our man waved and was seen. The ambulance then entered the cemetery and two paramedics rushed towards him and got him back on his feet without difficulty. A stretcher was unnecessary and he sat on a seat in the ambulance.

"And now, where do you want us to drive you?" "Well, to my house..." "Impossible, Sir, either we go to the hospital or to an institution empowered to receive you." "In that case the emergency department of the Grangettes Clinic, a few hundred metres away." "OK."

At the clinic, they put our old man onto a wheelchair until a doctor, who took his time coming, could examine him attentively before sending a diagnosis to his own general practitioner.

"There is no serious problem, you can go home now Sir."

Meanwhile, the young woman who wanted to plant the flowers on her father's grave was contacted and is not likely to forget this tragi-comical adventure. She accompanied our hero back to his car and he returned home.

Conclusion: a big thank you to the CPT insurance company who agreed to cover all the costs.

## Grandma and the Computer

*After deciding to enter the last one as a true (?) story I could not resist adding the following poem which despite everything above, I believe is probably not true:*

The computer swallowed Grandma,
Yes, honestly it's true!
She pressed Control and Enter,
And disappeared from view.

It devoured her completely,
The thought just makes me squirm.
She must have caught a virus,
Or been eaten by a worm.

I've searched the recycle bin,
And files of every kind,
I've even used the internet,
But nothing did I find.

At last I went to Google,
My searches to refine,
The reply from him was negative,
Not a thing was found online.

So, if inside your Inbox,
My Grandma you should see,
Please copy, scan and paste her,
And send her back to me.

## The Bounced Check

*The following is an actual letter that was sent to a bank by a 96-year-old woman. The bank manager thought it exceptional enough to have it published in the New York Times.*
*It is claimed to be true, but personally I cannot believe that it was done without assistance. We will never know.*

To whom it may concern,

I am writing to thank you for bouncing my check with which I endeavoured to pay my plumber last month. By my calculations three nanoseconds must have elapsed between his depositing the check and the arrival in my account of the funds needed to honor it. I refer of course, to the automatic monthly transfer of funds from my modest savings account, an arrangement which, I must admit has been in place for only thirty-one years.

You are to be commended for seizing that brief window of opportunity, and also for debiting my account by USD 30 by way of penalty for the inconvenience caused to your bank. My thankfulness springs from the manner in which this incident has caused me to rethink my errant financial ways. I noticed that whereas I personally attend to your telephone calls and letters, when I try to contact you, I am confronted by the impersonal, overcharging,  pre-recorded faceless entity which your bank has recently become.

From now on, I, like you, choose only to deal with a flesh-and-blood person. My mortgage and loan repayments will therefore and hereafter no longer be automatic, but will arrive at your bank by check, addressed personally and confidentially to an employee at your bank whom you must nominate. Be aware that it is an offence under the Postal Act for any other person to open such an envelope.

Please find attached an Application Contact Status form which I require your chosen employee to complete. I am sorry it runs to eight pages but in order that I know as much about him or her as your bank knows about me, there is no alternative. Please note that all copies of his or her medical history must be countersigned by a Notary Public, and the mandatory details of his/her financial situation (income, debts, assets and liabilities) must be accompanied by documented proof. In due course, I will issue your employee with a pin number which he/she must quote in dealings with me.

I regret that it cannot be shorter than 28 digits but, again, I have modeled it on the number of button presses required of me to access my account balance on your phone bank service.

As they say, imitation is the sincerest form of flattery.

Please allow me to level the playing field even further. When you call me, you will have a menu of options on my new voicemail system to choose from.

Please press the buttons as follows:

1. To make an appointment to see me
2. To query a missing payment
3. To transfer a call to my living room in case I am there
4. To transfer the call to my bedroom in case I am sleeping
5. To transfer the call to my toilet in case I am attending to nature
6. To transfer the call to my mobile phone in case I am not at home
7. To leave a message on my computer, a password to access my computer is required
8. Password will be communicated to you at a later date via the Authorised Contact
9. To return to the main menu to listen to options 1 through 7
10. To make a general complaint or inquiry. The contact will then be put on hold, pending the attention of my automatic answering service. While this may, on occasion, involve a lengthy wait, uplifting music will play for the duration of the call. Regrettably, but again following your example, i must also levy an establishment fee of USD 50 to cover the setting up of this new arrangement. Please credit my account after each occasion.

May I wish you a happy, if slightly less prosperous, New Year,

(signed)

Your Humble Client

*A favourite poem*

# *If*

by Rudyard Kipling
First published in the Brother Square-Toes chapter of Rewards and Fairies

If you can keep your head when all about you
Are losing theirs and blaming it on you.
If you can trust yourself when all men doubt you.
But make allowance for their doubting too.

If you can wait and not be tired by waiting.
Or being lied about, don't deal in lies,
Or being hated, don't give way to hating.
And yet don't look too good, nor talk too wise.

If you can dream – and not make dreams your master;
If you can think – and not make thoughts your aim:
If you can meet with triumph and disaster
And treat those two impostors just the same;
If you can bear to hear the truth you've spoken
Twisted by knaves to make a trap for fools
Or watch the things you gave your life to, broken.
And stoop and build 'em up with worn-out tools.
If you can make one heap of all your winnings

And risk it on one turn of pitch-and-toss.
And lose and start at your beginnings
And never breathe a word about your loss
If you can force your heart and nerve and sinew
To serve your turn long after they are gone
And so hold on when there is nothing in you
Except the Will which says to them, Hold on!

If you can talk with crowds and keep your virtue
Or walk with Kings – nor lose the common touch
If neither foes nor loving friends can hurt you
If all men count with you, but none too much
If you can fill the unforgiving minute
With sixty seconds worth of distance run
Yours is the Earth and everything that's in it
And – which is more – you'll be a Man, my son.

# CHAPTER 2 • TRUE LISTS

*My father had a close friend who spent all his career with the UK Pensions Office. When he retired and going through old papers, he came across – among many other things – a number of extracts of letters sent in to the Pensions Office. He collated them and sent the following list to my father.*

I cannot get sick pay. I have six children – can you tell me why this is?

This is my eighth child – what are you going to do about it?

Mrs. R. has no clothes and has not had any for a year. The clergy have been visiting her.

I am forwarding my marriage certificate and two children, one of which is a mistake – as you can see.

In reply to your letter, I have already co-habited with your office so far without result.

Sir, I am glad to say that my husband reported missing is now dead.

Unless I get my husband's money I will be forced to lead an immortal life.

I am writing these lines for Mrs. G. who cannot write herself – she expects to be confined next week and can do with it.

I am sending you my marriage certificate and six children. I had seven, and one died which was baptised on half a sheet of paper by Rev. Thomas.

Please find out if my husband is dead as the man I am living with now won't eat or do anything until he is sure.

In answer to your letter I have given birth to a little boy weighing 10 pounds. Is this satisfactory?

You have changed my little girl into a little boy – will this make any difference?

Please send my money at once as I have fallen into errors with my landlord.

I have no children as my husband is a bus driver and works all day and night.

In accordance with your instructions I have given birth to twins in the enclosed envelope.

I want money quick as you can send it. I have been in bed with the doctor all week and he does not seem to be doing me any good.

RE your enquiry, the teeth in the top are alright, but the ones in my bottom are hurting horribly.

## "This is the Captain speaking"

*There is unfortunately an increasing tendency for in-flight passenger announcements in the air to be given on pre-recorded switch-ons. I say unfortunately because most frequent flyers hear the same cold repetitive statements over and over again. How refreshing to have a home-made announcement from someone who has just buckled up your belt. Here is something of what we risk losing, at least in entertainment.*

1. On a Continental air flight with very "senior" flight attendants, came a declaration from the pilot: "Ladies and gentlemen, we have reached cruising altitude and will be turning down the cabin lights. This is for your comfort and to enhance the appearance of your flight attendants." *(What might have happened to him after the plane landed!)*
2. After landing a stewardess said, "Please be sure to take all your belongings. If you're going to leave anything, please make sure it is something we'd like to have."
3. "There may be fifty ways to leave your lover, but there are only four ways out of this aircraft.
4. "Thank you for flying Delta Business Express. We hope you enjoyed giving us the business as much as we enjoyed taking you for a ride."
5. As the plane landed and was coming to a stop at the gate at Washington National, a lone voice came over the loudspeaker, "Whoa, big fella, Whoa."
6. After a particularly rough landing during thunderstorms in Memphis, a flight attendant on a Northwest flight announced, "Please take care when opening the overhead compartments because after a landing like that, sure as hell everything has shifted."
7. From a Southwest airlines employee, "Welcome aboard the Southwest flight from xxx to yyy. To operate your seat belt insert the metal tab into the buckle and pull tight. It works just like every other seat belt and if you don't know how to operate one you probably shouldn't be out in public unsupervised."
8. In the event of a sudden loss of cabin pressure, masks will descend from the ceiling. Stop screaming, grab the mask, and pull it over your face. If you have a small child travelling with you, secure your mask before assisting with theirs. If you are travelling with more than one small child……..pick your favourite.

9.  Weather at our destination is 50 degrees with some broken clouds, but we'll fix them before we arrive. Thank you, and remember, nobody loves you and your money more than Southwest Airlines.

10. Your seat cushions can be used for flotation; and in the event of an emergency water landing, please paddle to shore and take them with our compliments.

11. Should the cabin lose pressure, oxygen masks will drop from the overhead area. Please place the bag over your own mouth and nose before assisting children, or other adults acting like children.

12. As you exit the plane, make sure you gather all of your belongings. Anything left over will be distributed evenly among the flight attendants. Please do not leave children or spouses.

13. And from the pilot during his welcome message "Delta Airlines is pleased to have some of the best flight attendants in the industry. Unfortunately none of them are on this flight." *(Wait and you'll get a reaction after landing, see under Quote 1)*

14. Heard on Southwest Airlines after a very hard landing in Salt Lake City: the flight attendant came on the telecom and said, "That was quite a bump and I know what y'all thinking. I'm here to tell you it wasn't the airline's fault, it wasn't the pilot's fault, it wasn't the flight attendant's fault, it was the asphalt."

15. Overheard on an American Airlines flight into Amarillo, Texas on a particularly windy and bumpy day. During the final approach, the Captain was really having to fight it. After an extremely bumpy landing, the flight attendant said, "Ladies and gentlemen, welcome to Amarillo. Please remain with your seat belts fastened while the Captain taxies in what's left of our airplane."

16. A flight attendant's comment on a less than perfect landing: "Please remain seated while Captain Kangaroo taxies us in."

17. An airline pilot wrote that on this particular flight he had hammered his ship into the runway really hard. The airline had a policy which required the first officer to stand in the doorway while the passengers left, smile and say, "Thanks for flying with XYZ airline." He said that because of the bad landing he had a hard time looking the passengers in the eye, thinking that someone would react with a smart comment. Finally there was only a little old lady walking with a cane. She said, "Sonny, mind if I ask you a question?" "Why, no, Madam," replied the pilot. "Tell me," the little old lady asked, "Did we land or were we shot down?"

## *Airline stories – taken from travel agents*

A nice lady just called. She needed to know how it was possible that her flight from Detroit left at 8:20 am and got into Chicago at 8:33 am. I tried to explain that Michigan was an hour ahead of Illinois, but she could not understand the concept of time zones. Finally I told her the plane went very fast, and she bought that!

A woman called and asked, "Do airlines put your physical description on your bag so they know who's luggage belongs to who?"
I said, "No, why do you ask?"
She replied, "Well, when I checked in with the airline, they put a tag on my luggage that said FAT, and as I'm overweight, is there any connection?"
After putting her on hold for a minute while "I looked into it" (I was actually laughing) I came back and explained that the city code for Fresno is FAT, and that the airline was just putting a destination tag on her luggage.

I just got off the phone with a man who asked, "How do I know which plane to get on?"
I asked him what exactly he meant, to which he replied, "I was told my flight number is 823, but none of these darn planes have numbers on them."

A woman called and said, "I need to fly to Pepsi-Cola on one of these computer planes."
I asked if she meant to fly to Pensacola on a commuter plane. She said, "Yeah, whatever."

A business man called and had a question about the documents he needed in order to fly
to China. After a lengthy discussion about passports, I reminded him he needed a visa.
"Oh no I don't, I've been to China many times and never had to have one of those."
I double checked and sure enough, his stay required a visa. When I told him this he said,
"Look, I've been to China four times and every time they've accepted my American Express."

A woman called to make reservations, "I want to go from Chicago to Hippopotamus, New York".
The agent was at loss for words, and finally managed to ask, "Are you sure that's the name of the town?"
"Yes, what flights do you have?" replied the customer.
After some searching, the agent came back with, "I'm sorry, ma'am, I've looked up every airport code in the country and can't find a Hippopotamus anywhere."
The customer retorted, "Oh, don't be silly. Everyone knows where it is. Check your map!"
He scoured a map of the state of New York and finally offered;
"You don't mean Buffalo, do you?"
"That's it! I knew it was a big animal."

## Insults with Class

*I have the impression that in today's world, insults are more brutal, more raw, more blunt, but much less subtle and therefore less effective. They used to contain humour and sarcasm and were therefore more quotable, as one can see from the following:*

*Abraham Lincoln (1809-1865)*
He can compress the most words into the smallest idea of any man
I know.

*John Bright (1811-1889)*
He is a self-made man and worships his creator.

*Mark Twain (1835-1918)*
I didn't attend the funeral, but I sent a nice letter saying
that I approved of it.
Why do you sit there like an envelope without any address on it?

*Oscar Wilde (1854-1910)*
He has no enemies but is intensely disliked by his friends.

*Winston Churchill (1875-1956)*
He has all the virtues I dislike and none of the virtues I admire.

*George-Bernard Shaw (1856-1950)*
I am enclosing two tickets fort he first night of my new play; bring a friend, if you have one.

*Winston Churchill (1875-1956)*
Cannot possibly attend the first night, will attend the second ... if there is one.

*Clarence Darrow (1857-1938)*
I have never killed a man, but I have read many obituaries with great pleasure.

*Groucho Marx (1890-1977)*
I've had a perfectly wonderful evening, but this wasn't it.

*Moses Hadas (1900-1977)*
Thank you for sending me a copy of your book. I'll waste no time reading it.

*Jack E. Leonard (1910-1977*
There is nothing wrong with you that reincarnation won't cure.

## Hotels

*and other tourist attractions which have notices. Why don't they get a translator?*
*(I'm glad they don't or this list would be non-existent.)*

Tokyo – "Is forbidden to steal hotel towels please. If you are not a person to do such a thing, please not to read."

Bucharest – in the lobby - "The lift is being fixed for the next day. During that time we regret that you will be unbearable."

Leipzig – elevator – "Do not enter the lift backwards, and only when lit up."

Paris – elevator –"Please leave your values at the front desk."

Athens – "Visitors are expected to complain between the hours of 9 am and 11 am daily."

Yugoslavia – "The flattening of underwear with pleasure is the job of the chambermaid."

Japan – "You are invited to take advantage of the chambermaid." *(Did DSK really think he was in Japan --- he never said so)*

Moscow – lobby – opposite the Russian Orthodox Monastery – "You are welcome to visit the cemetery where Russian and Soviet composers, artists and writers are buried daily except Thursday."

Austria – ski resort –."Not to perambulate in the hours of repose in the boots of ascension."

Switzerland – restaurant menu – "Our wines leave you with nothing to hope for."

Poland – menu – "Salads a firm's own make; limpid red beet soup with cheesy dumplings in the form of a finger; roasted duck let loose; beef rashers beaten up in the country people's fashion."

Hong Kong – tailor shop – "Ladies may have a fit upstairs."

Bangkok – dry cleaners – "Drop your trousers off for best results."

Moscow (Soviet Weekly) – "There will be a Moscow exhibition of Arts by 15,000 Soviet Republic painters and sculptors. These were executed over the past two years."

Germany – Black Forest – "It is strictly forbidden on our Black Forest camping site that people of different sex, for instance, men and women, live together in one tent unless they are married with each other for that purpose."

Zurich – "Because of the impropriety of entertaining guests of the opposite sex in the bedroom, it is suggested that the lobby be used for this purpose."

Hong Kong – dentist – "Teeth extracted by the latest Methodists."

Rome – laundry – "Ladies, leave your clothes here and spend the afternoon having a good time."

Czechoslovakia – tourist agency – "Take one of our horse driven city tours – we guarantee no miscarriages."

Thailand – donkey rides – "Would you like to ride on your own ass?"

Switzerland – a mountain inn – "Special today – no ice cream."

Bangkok temple – "It is forbidden to enter a women, even a foreigner dressed as a man."

Copenhagen airline ticket office – "We take your bags and send them in all directions."

Moscow hotel room – "If this is your first visit to the USSR, you are welcome to it."

Norwegian cocktail lounge – "Ladies are requested not to have babies in the bar."

Budapest zoo – "Please do not feed the animals. If you have any suitable food give it to the guard on duty."

Acapulco hotel – "The manager has personally passed all the water served here."

Tokyo shop – "Our nylons cost more than common but you will find they are the best in the long run."

Tokyo car rental firm – "When a passenger of foot heave in sight, tootle the horn. Trumpet him melodiously at first, but he still obstacles your passage, then tootle him with vigour."

Belgrade elevator – "To move the cabin. Pushbutton for wishing floor. If the cabin should enter more persons, each one should press a number of wishing floor."

Tokyo bar – "Special cocktails for ladies with nuts."

Rome doctor's office – "Specialist in women and other diseases."

Japanese information booklet – "Air conditioner – Cooles and heates: if you want just condition warm in your room, please control yourself."

Majorca shop entrance – "English well talking. Here speeching American."

Paris dress shop – "Dresses for street-walking."

Rhodes – tailor shop – "Order your summers suit. Because is big rush we will execute customers in strict rotation."

## ACTUAL NEWSPAPER HEADLINES COLLECTED BY A GROUP OF JOURNALISTS

*(In the following list in many of the titles the double meaning is not immediately apparent and for a variety of reasons, so it is better to read it either slowly or at intervals)*

Something Went Wrong in Jet Crash, Expert Says

Police Begin Campaign to Run Down Jaywalkers

Safety Experts say School Bus Passengers Should Be Belted

Drunk gets Nine Months in Violin Case *(period of gestation?)*

Survivor of Siamese Twins Joins Parents

Farmer Bill Dies in House

Iraqi Head Seeks Arms

Is there a Ring of Debris around Uranus?

Stud Tires Out

Prostitutes Appeal to Pope

Panda Mating Fails; Veterinarian Takes Over

Soviet Virgin Lands Short of Goal again

British left Waffles on Falkland Isles

Lung Cancer in Women Mushrooms

Eye Drops On shelf.

Teacher Strikes Idle Kids

Reagan Wins on Budget, but More Lies Ahead

Squad Helps Dog Bite Victim

Shot Off Women's Leg Helps Nicklaus to 66

Enraged Cow Injures Farmer with Axe

Plane Too Close to Ground, Crash Probe Told

Miners Refuse to Work after Death

Juvenile Court to Try Shooting Defendant

Stolen Painting Found by Tree

Two Soviet Ships Collide, One Dies

Two Sisters Reunited after 18 years in Checkout Counter

Killer Sentenced to Die for Second Time in 10 years

Never Withhold Herpes Infection from Loved One

Drunken Drivers Paid USD 1000 in '84 War Dims Hope for Peace

If Strike isn't Settled Quickly it May Last a While

Cold Wave Linked to Temperatures

Enfield Couple Slain. Police suspect Homicide

Red Tape Holds Up New Bridge

Deer Kill 17000

Typhoon Rips through Cemetery – Hundreds Dead

Man Struck by Lightning Faces Battery Charge

New Study of Obesity Looks for Larger Test Groups

Astronaut takes Blame for Gas in Spacecraft

Kids Make Nutritious Snacks

Chef Throws his Heart into Feeding Needy

Arson Suspect Held in Massachusetts Fire

British Union Finds Dwarfs in Short Supply

Ban on Soliciting Dead in Trotwood

Lansing Residents Can Drop Off Trees

Local High School Dropouts Cut in Half

New Vaccine May Contain Rabies

Man Minus Ear Waives Hearing

Deaf College Opens Doors to Hearing

Air Head Fired

Steals Clock, Faces Time

Prosecutor Releases Probe into Undersherriff

Old School Pillars are Replaced by Alumni

Bank Drive-in Window Blocked by Board

Hospitals are Sued by 7 Foot Doctors

Some Pieces of Rock Hudson Sold at Auction

Sex Education Delayed, Teachers Request Training

Include Your Children when Baking Cookies

## At the Law Courts

*Most litigation lawyers work on a number of systems or strategies facilitating a line of questioning in court and ensuring that they cover all the aspects of a specific situation. The concept is excellent but has some weaknesses when the line of questioning accidentally crosses over the line of logic. The results of these hiccups have become very popular and have often been quoted, so although many readers will have come across the following examples this is not a reason to exclude them from my collection.. Lawyers typically aren't funny, unless by accident. Not all have this problem but one or two show up the imprecision of the development of language: all these following were taken from official US court records nationwide.*

Q. Are you sexually active?
A. No, I just lie there.

Q. *What is your date of birth?*
A. *15th July.*
Q. *What year?*
A. *Every year.*

Q. What gear were you in at the moment of impact?
A. Gucci sweats and Reeboks.

Q. *This myasthenia gravis, does it affect your memory at all?*
A. *Yes.*
Q. *And in what ways does it affect your memory?*
A. *I forget.*
Q. *You forget. Can you give us an example of something you've forgotten?*

Q. How old is your son, the one living with you?
A. Thirty eight or thirty five, I can't remember which.
Q. How long has he lived with you?
A. Forty-five years.

Q. *What was the first thing your husband said to you when he woke up that morning?*
A. *He said, "Where am I, Cathy?"*
Q. *And why did that upset you?*
A. *My name is Susan.*

Q. The youngest son, the twenty-year-old, how old is he?

Q. *You don't know what it was, and you didn't know what it looked like, but can you describe it?*

Q. Do you know if your daughter has ever been involved in voodoo or the occult?

A. We both do.

Q. Voodoo?

A. We do.

Q. You do?

A. Yes, voodoo.

Q. *Now doctor, isn't it true that when a person dies in his sleep, he doesn't know about it until the morning?*

A. *Did you actually pass your bar exam?*

Q. Do you know how many months pregnant you are now?

A. I'll be three months on November 8th.

Q. So the date of conception (of the baby) was August 8th?

A Yes.

Q. And what were you doing at that time?

Q. *She had three children, right?*

A. *Yes.*

Q. *How Many were boys?*

A. *None.*

Q. *Were there any girls?*

Q. How was your first marriage terminated?

A. By death.

A. And by whose death was it terminated?

Q. *Can you describe the individual?*

A. *He was about medium height and had a beard.*

Q. *Was this a male or a female?*

Q. Is your appearance here this morning pursuant to a deposition notice which I sent to your attorney?

A. No this is how I dress when I go to work,

Q. *Doctor, how many autopsies have you performed on dead people?*

A. *All my autopsies are performed on dead people.*

Q. All your responses must be oral.

A. OK.

Q. What school did you go to?

A. Oral.

*Q. Do you recall the time at which you examined the body of Mr. Dennington at the Rose Chapel?*
*A. It was in the evening. The autopsy started around 8.30 pm.*
*Q. And Mr. Dennington was dead at the time, is that correct?*
*A. No, you stupid oaf, he was sitting on the table wondering why I was doing an autopsy.*

Q. Are you qualified to give a urine sample?
A. Huh?

*Q. Doctor, before you performed the autopsy, did you check for a pulse?*
*A. No.*
*Q. Did you check for blood pressure?*
*A. No.*
*Q. did you check for breathing?*
*A. No.*
*Q. So, then it is possible that the patient was alive when you began the autopsy?*
*A. No.*
*Q. But how can you be so sure, Doctor?*
*A. Because his brain was sitting in a jar on my desk.*
*Q. But could the patient still have been alive nevertheless?*
*A. Yes, it is possible that he could have been alive and practising law somewhere.*

Q. What happened then?
A. He told me, he says, "I have to kill you because you can identify me!"
Q. Did he kill you?

*Q. Was it you or your brother that was killed in the war?*

Q. Were you alone or by yourself?

*Q. Do you have any children or anything of that kind?*

Q. I show you Exhibit 3 and ask you if you recognise that picture.
A. That's me.
Q. Were you present when the picture was taken?
A. Would you repeat the question?

*Q. Have you lived in this town all your life?*
*A. Not yet.*

## *Out of the Mouths of Babes and Sucklings*

*HOW DO YOU DECIDE WHO TO MARRY?*

You got to find somebody who likes the same stuff. Like if you like sports, she should like it that you like sports, and she should keep the chips and dip coming. – Alan, age 10.

No person really decides before they grow up who they're going to marry. God decides it all, way before, and you get to find out later who you're stuck with. – Kirsten, age 10.

*WHAT IS THE RIGHT AGE TO GET MARRIED?*

Twenty-three is the best age because you know the person forever by then. – Camille, age 10.

No age is good to get married at. You got to be a fool to get married. – Freddie age 6.

*HOW CAN A STRANGER TELL IF TWO PEOPLE ARE MARRIED?*

Married people usually look happy to talk to other people. – Eddie, age 6.

You might have to guess, based on whether they seem to be yelling at the same kids. – Derrick, age 8.

*WHAT DO YOU THINK YOUR MOM AND DAD HAVE IN COMMON?*

Both don't want no more kids. – Lori. Age 8.

*WHAT DO MOST PEOPLE DO ON A DATE?*

Dates are having fun, and people should use them to get to know each other. Even boys have something to say if you listen long enough. – Lynette, age 8.

On the first date, they just tell each other lies, and that usually gets them interested enough to go for a second date. – Martin, age 10.

*WHAT WOULD YOU DO ON A FIRST DATE THAT WAS TURNING SOUR?*

I'd run home and play dead. The next day I would call all the newspapers and make sure they wrote about me in all the dead columns. – Craig, age 9.

*WHEN IS IT OK TO KISS SOMEONE?*

When they're rich. – Pam, age 7.

The law says you have to be eighteen, so I wouldn't want to mess with that. – Curt, age 10.

The rule is: if you kiss someone, then you should marry them and have kids with them. It's the right thing to do
– Howard, age 8.

*IS IT BETTER TO BE SINGLE OR MARRIED?*

It's better for girls to be single but not for boys. Boys need someone to clean up after them. – Anita, age 9.

Single is better, for a simple reason that I wouldn't want to change no diapers. Of course, if I did get married, I'd just phone my mother and have her come over for some coffee and diaper-changing.
– Kirsten, age 10.

*HOW WOULD THE WORLD BE DIFFERENT IF PEOPLE DIDN'T GET MARRIED?*

There sure would be a lot of kids to explain away, wouldn't there?
– Kelvin, age 8.

*HOW WOULD YOU MAKE A MARRIAGE WORK?*

Tell your wife that she looks pretty even if she looks like a truck.
– Ricky, age 10.

## A Scottish farmer...

*One of my favourites. This story appears now unfortunately to be untrue as claimed by Sir Alexander Fleming's biographer, Kevin Brown. Also Fleming is supposed to have called it a wrong version.*

His name was Fleming and he was a poor Scottish farmer. One day while working on the land trying to make a living for his family, he heard a cry for help coming from a nearby bog. He dropped his tools and ran to the bog. There mired to his waist in the black muck, was a terrified boy, screaming and struggling to free himself. Farmer Fleming freed the lad from what would have been a slow and terrifying death.

The next day a fancy carriage drew up outside the Scotsman's sparse cottage. An elegantly dressed nobleman stepped out of the carriage and Introduced himself as the father of the boy Farmer Fleming had saved.

"I want to repay you" said the nobleman "You saved my son's life."

"No I can't accept payment for what I did," the Scottish farmer replied, waving off the offer.

At that moment, the farmer's own son came to the door of the family hovel. "Is that your son?" the nobleman asked.

"Yes," the farmer replied proudly.

"I'll make you a deal. Let me provide him with the level of education my son will enjoy. If the lad is anything like his father, he'll no doubt grow to be a man we will both be proud of."

And that he did. Farmer Fleming's son attended the very best schools and, in time, he graduated from St. Mary's Hospital Medical School in London and went on to become known throughout the world as the noted Sir Alexander Fleming, the discoverer of penicillin.

Years afterward, the same nobleman's son who had been saved from the bog, was stricken with pneumonia. What saved his life this time? PENICILLIN.

The name of the nobleman? Lord Randolph Churchill. His son's name? Winston Churchill.

*Girl with an Apple*

## A STORY ONLY BASED ON TRUTH

*Piotrkow, Poland, August 1942*

The sky was gloomy that morning as we waited anxiously. All the men, women and children of Piotrkow's Jewish community had been herded into a square. Word had got around that we were being moved. My father had only recently died from typhus, which had run rampant through the crowded ghetto. My greatest fear was that our family would be separated.

"Whatever you do," Isidore, my eldest brother, whispered to me, "don't tell them your age. Say that you are sixteen." I was tall for a boy of eleven, so I could pull it off. That way I might be deemed valuable as a worker.

An SS man approached me, boots clicking against the cobblestones. He looked me up and down, and then asked my age. My mother was motioned to the right with the other women, children, sick and elderly people.

I whispered to Isidore "Why?" He didn't answer. I ran to Mama's side and said I wanted to stay with her.

"No," she said sternly. "Get away. Don't be a nuisance. Go with your brothers."

She had never spoken to me so harshly before. But I understood. She was protecting me. She loved me so much that, just this once, she pretended not to. It was the last I ever saw of her.

My brothers and I were transported in a cattle car to Germany. We arrived at the Buchenwald concentration camp one night weeks later and were led into a crowded barrack. The next day we were issued uniforms and identification numbers. "Don't call me Herman any more," I said to my brothers, "Call me 94983." I was put to work in the camp's crematorium, loading the dead into a hand-cranked elevator. I, too, felt dead. Hardened, I had become a number. Soon, my brothers and I were sent to Schlieben, one of Buchenwald's sub-camps near Berlin.

One morning I thought I heard my mother's voice... "Son," she said, softly but clearly. "I am going to send you an angel." Then I woke up. Just a dream. A beautiful dream. But in this place there could be no angels.

There was only work. And hunger. And fear.

A couple of days later I was walking around the camp, around the barracks, near the barbed-wire fence where the guards could not easily see. I was alone. On the other side of the fence I spotted someone: a little girl with light, almost luminous curls. She was half-hidden behind a birch tree. I glanced around to make sure no one saw me. I called to her softly in German "Do you have something to eat?" She didn't understand. I inched closer to the fence and repeated the question in Polish. I was thin and gaunt, with rags wrapped around my feet, but the girl looked unafraid. In her eyes I saw life.

She pulled an apple from her woollen jacket and threw it over the fence. I grabbed the fruit and, as I started to run away, I heard her say faintly, "I'll see you tomorrow." I returned to the same spot by the fence every day. She was always there with something for me to eat – a hunk of bread or better still an apple.

We didn't dare speak or linger. To be caught would be death for us both. I didn't know anything about her, just a kind farm girl, except that she understood Polish. What was her name? Why was she risking her life for me? Hope was in such short supply, and this girl on the other side of the fence gave me some, as nourishing as the bread and apples.

Nearly seven months later my brothers and I were crammed into a coal car and shipped to the Theresienstadt camp in Czechoslovakia. "Don't return," I told the girl that day. "We're leaving." I turned toward the barracks and didn't look back, didn't even say goodbye to the little girl whose name I'd never learned, the girl with the apples.

We were in Theresienstadt for three months. The war was winding down and the allied forces were closing in, yet my fate seemed sealed. On May 10th 1945, I was scheduled to die in the gas chamber at 10.00 am. In the quiet of dawn I tried to prepare myself. So many times death seemed ready to claim me, but somehow I'd survived. Now it was over. I thought of my parents. At least, I thought, we will be re-united. But at 8 am there was a commotion. I heard shouts and saw people running every which way through the camp. I caught up with my brothers.

Russian troops had liberated the camp! The gates swung open. Everyone was running so I did too. Amazingly all my brothers had survived. I'm not sure how but I knew that the girl with the apples was the key to my survival. In a place where evil seemed triumphant, one person's goodness had saved my life, had given me hope in a place where there was none. My mother had promised to send me an angel and the angel had come.

Eventually, I made my way to England where I was sponsored by a Jewish charity, put up in a hostel with other boys who had survived the Holocaust, and trained in electronics. Then I came to America, where my brother Sam had already moved. I served in the US Army during the Korean War, and returned to New York City after two years. By 1957, I had opened my own electronics repair shop. I was starting to settle in.

One day, my friend, Sid whom I knew from England, called me, "I've got a date. She's got a Polish friend. Let's double date." A blind date? No, that wasn't for me. But Sid kept pestering me, and a few days later we headed up to the Bronx to pick up his date and her friend, Roma. I had to admit, for a blind date, this wasn't so bad. Roma was a nurse at a Bronx hospital. She was kind and smart. Beautiful too, with swirling brown curls and green almond shaped eyes that sparkled with life. The four of us drove out to Coney Island. Roma was easy to talk to, easy to be with. It turned out that she was wary of blind dates too! We were both just doing our friends a favour. We took a stroll along the broad-walk, enjoying the salty Atlantic breeze and then had dinner by the shore. I couldn't remember having a better time. We piled back into Sid's car, Roma and I sharing the back seat.

As European Jews who had survived the war, we were aware that much had been left unsaid between us. She broached the subject "Where were you during the war?" she asked softly "The camps." I said. The terrible memories still vivid, the irreparable loss I had tried to forget. But you can never forget., She nodded, "My family was hiding on a farm in Germany, not far from Berlin," she told me "My father knew a priest, and he got us Aryan papers.

I imagined how she must have suffered too, fear a constant companion, and yet, here we were, both survivors in a new world. "There was a camp near the farm," Roma continued,

"I saw a boy there and I would throw him apples every day." What an amazing coincidence that she had helped some other boy! "What did he look like?" I asked. "He was tall, skinny and hungry. I must have seen him every day for six months." My heart was racing. I couldn't believe it. This couldn't be. "Did he tell you one day not to come back because he was leaving Schlieben?" Roma looked at me, amazed, "Yes." "That was me!"

I was ready to burst with joy and awe, flooded with emotions, I couldn't believe it! My angel. "I'm not letting you go," I told her. And there in the back of the car, I proposed to her. I couldn't wait. "You're crazy!" she said. But she invited me to meet her parents the next week.

There was so much to look forward to learning about Roma, but the most important things I already knew: her steadfast-ness and her goodness. For many months in the worst of circumstances, she had come to the fence and given me hope. Now that I'd found her again, I could never let her go.

That day she said yes. And I kept my word. After nearly fifty years of marriage, two children and three grandchildren, I have never let her go.

Herman Rosenblat of Miami Beach, Florida.


*28.11.2008 --- I received this story with the information that it was to be made into a film called "The Fence."*

*20.12.2008 --- His publisher acknowledges that he accepted that the key portion of the memoir, that of the meeting with his wife at the camp, was a fake.*
*2009 --- The "Love Story" aspect with his wife Roma is accepted as being completely fabricated. Later, he stated, "In my imagination, in my mind, I believed it was true."*

## Nuts and Bolts

*I heard the following story many decades ago and it was told as dating from the 1920s when motor cars were less reliable than today and breakdowns and tyre problems were not infrequent. Many claim that it is not true. I would like to think it is, anyway it's good enough for that not to be of great importance.*

One such case was a car that had a tyre puncture and needed to a wheel change. Three men poured out of the car which had been pulled into the side of the road alongside a wall. On the wall sat a man with a broad smile kicking his legs against the wall and obviously enjoying the scene immensely.

"Is there a garage nearby? As you can see we have just had a puncture and none of us are very good at this sort of thing."

"I'm afraid not. You see this place is right out in the middle of the country all on its own because it is a lunatic asylum."

"Oh, well, maybe if you have a car we could borrow it to go and get a mechanic. You can see our predicament and we have never changed a wheel before."

The man on the wall gave a high-pitched screech of laughter and went on swinging his legs, "I'm not a member of the staff, I'm a patient having treatment but they all tell me I am not dangerous, just crazy. Furthermore it's Sunday and no one is around."

The three friends shrugged their shoulders and pooled their resources to make the best of a bad job. The man on the wall went on swinging his legs and making occasional very irritating remarks interspersed with chuckles. The men found the instruction book, found the jack and other tools and managed to undo the four bolts holding the wheel, took the wheel off and started to put the spare wheel in its place. But where are the bolts? Our man on the wall gave a great shout of glee "Did you not see? As you took off the bolts, you threw them on one side and they rolled down the drain ---- lost and gone forever."

Absolute disaster !!! The man who had been doing all the work, by now extremely irritated, shouted "You're so clever sitting up there making comments on everything we do. Why don't you say something sensible for once. We're in a real mess. We're stuck here until we get outside help."

The man on the wall said "Why don't you take one bolt from each of the other wheels and use them for your new wheel? That will give you three bolts on each of the four wheels. Then when you get to a garage you can buy four new bolts."

There was a silence: the men were dumbstruck. Then one said "That's absolutely brilliant. How is it you can come up with something like this?"
The man on the wall replied, "Look, I may be crazy, but I'm not STUPID!!!"

# CHAPTER 4 • STORIES

## *Miss Beatrice*

The church organist was in her eighties and had never been married. She was admired for her sweetness and kindness to all.

One afternoon the pastor came to call on her and she showed him into her quaint sitting room. She invited him to have a seat.

While he sat facing her old Hammond organ, the young minister noticed a cut glass bowl sitting on top of it. The bowl was filled with water, and in the water floated, of all things, a condom!

When she returned with tea and scones, they began to chat. The pastor tried to stifle his curiosity about the bowl of water and its strange floater, but soon it got the better of him and he could no longer resist. "Miss Beatrice," he said, "I wonder if you would tell me about this?" pointing to the bowl.

"Oh yes," she replied, "Isn't it wonderful?" I was walking through the park a few months ago and I found this little package on the ground. The directions said to place it on the organ, keep it wet and that it would prevent the spread of disease. Do you know I haven't had the 'flu all winter?"

## How to know you are growing older...

Everything hurts and what doesn't hurt, doesn't work.

The gleam in your eye is the sun hitting your bifocals.

You feel like the night before and you haven't been anywhere.

Your little black book contains only names ending in M.D.

You get winded playing cards.

Your children begin to look middle-aged.

You join a health club and don't go.

A dripping tap causes an uncontrollable bladder urge.

You know all the answers, but nobody asks the questions.

You look forward to a dull evening.

You need glasses to find your glasses.
You turn out the lights for economic rather than romantic reasons.
You sit in a rocking chair and can't get it going.
Your knees buckle but your belt won't.
Your back goes out more than you do.
You have too much room in the house and enough in the medicine chest.
You sink your teeth in a steak and they stay there.
You wonder why more people don't use this size print.

### The Coke Salesman in Israel

A disappointed salesman of Coca-Cola returned from his assignment to Israel.

A friend asked, "Why weren't you successful with the Israelis?"

The salesman explained, "When I got posted, I was very confident that I would make a good sales pitch. But I had a problem. I didn't know how to speak Hebrew. So I planned to convey the message through three posters.

**First poster**: A man lying in the hot desert sand totally exhausted and fainting.
**Second poster**: The man is drinking Coca-Cola.
**Third poster**: Our man is now totally refreshed.

And then these posters were pasted all over the place.

"Terrific idea! That should have worked!" said the friend.

"The hell it should have!" said the salesman.

"But no one told me they read from right to left!"

1

### The Gravy Ladle

*An elderly priest invited a young priest over for dinner. During the meal, the young priest couldn't help noticing how attractive and shapely the housekeeper was.*

*Over the course of the evening he started to wonder if there was more between the elderly priest and the housekeeper than met the eye. Reading the young priest's thoughts, the elderly priest volunteered, "I know what you must be thinking, but I assure you, my relationship with my housekeeper is purely professional."*

*About a week later the housekeeper came to the elderly priest and said, "Father, ever since the young Father came to dinner, I've been unable to find the beautiful silver gravy ladle. You don't suppose he took it do you?"*

*The priest answered, "Well, I doubt it, but I'll write him a letter just to be sure."*

*So he sat down and wrote: "Dear Father, I'm not saying that you 'did' take a gravy ladle from my house, and I am not saying you 'did not' take a gravy ladle. But the fact remains that one has been missing ever since you were here for dinner.*

*Several days later the elderly priest received a letter from the young priest which read: "Dear Father, I'm not saying that you 'do' sleep with your housekeeper, and I'm not saying that you 'do not' sleep with your housekeeper. But the fact remains that if you were sleeping in your own bed, you would have found the gravy ladle by now."*

*From my father's collection – one of his favourites*

## Aggie the Bricklayer

TO: AETNA INSURANCE COMPANY

I am writing in response to your request for additional information. On line 3 of the accident report form, I wrote that "Cause of accident was poor planning." You said I should explain in more detail. I trust the following will be sufficient:

I am a bricklayer by trade. On the day of the accident, I was working alone on the roof of a new six story building. When I completed my work, I discovered that I had about 500 pounds of bricks left over. Rather than carry the bricks down by hand, I decided to lower them down in a barrel by using a pulley which was attached to the side of the building.

Securing the rope at ground level, I went up to the roof, swung the barrel out, and loaded the bricks into it. Then I went back to the ground and untied the rope, holding it tightly to ensure a slow descent of the 500 pounds of bricks. (You will note on line 11 that I weigh 135 pounds).

Due to my surprise at being jerked off the ground so suddenly, I lost my presence of mind and forgot to let go of the rope. Needless to say I proceeded at a rather rapid rate up the side of the building. In the vicinity of the third floor, I met the barrel coming down. This explains the fractured skull and broken collarbone.

Slowed only slightly, I continued my rapid ascent, not stopping until the fingers of my right hand were two knuckles deep into the pulley. Fortunately by this time I had regained my presence of mind, and was able to hold tightly to the rope in spite of the pain.

At approximately the same time however, the barrel of bricks hit the ground and the bottom fell out of the barrel. Relieved of the weight of the bricks, the barrel now weighed approximately 50 pounds.

I refer you again to my own weight set out on line 11. As you might imagine I was unable to stand or move, and watching the empty barrel six stories above me, I again lost my presence of mind and let go of the rope...

I began to fall, and I met the barrel coming up. This accounts for the two fractured ankles and the lacerations on my legs and buttocks.

The encounter with the barrel slowed me up enough to lessen my injuries when I fell onto the pile of bricks. Fortunately only three of my vertebrae were cracked.

I am sorry to report however, that as I lay there on the bricks, in much pain, unable to stand or move, and watching the empty barrel six stories above me, I again lost my presence of mind and let go of the rope...

P.S.     My mother is typing this letter in my hospital room.

P.P.S.   I think I got the carbon in backwards (Aggie's mom).

## Guessing game

Once upon a time a shepherd was herding his large flock of sheep just off the edge of a deserted dirt road. Suddenly a brand new Jeep Cherokee screeched to a halt next to him. The driver, a young man dressed in a Brioni suit, Cerrutti shoes, Ray-Ban glasses, and a YSL tie got out and asked, "If I guess how many sheep you have, will you give me one of them?"

The shepherd looked at the young man, then at the sheep which grazed as far as he could see and said, "OK."

The young man re-entered his car, connected his laptop and the mobile, entered a NASA site; then scanned the ground using his GPS, opened a data base and 60 Excel tables filled with algorithms, then printed a five-page report on his high-tech mini printer. After, a quick scan of the report, he turned to the shepherd and said: "You have exactly 1,586 sheep here."

"That's correct, you can have your sheep," answered the shepherd. The young man picked up his choice and put it in the back of his jeep.

The shepherd asked him, "If I guess your profession, will you give it back to me?"

The young man smiled and said "Sure, why not?"

Without hesitating the shepherd said "You are an Arthur Anderson or KPMG consultant!"

"KPMG, but how did you know?" asked the young man.

"Very simple," answered the shepherd. "First, you come here uninvited ; second, you charged me to tell me something I already knew and third, you do not know my business, because you just put my dog in your jeep!"

COLLEGE OF FINE ARTS, ALBANY N.Y.

Dear Mother and Dad,

It has now been three months since I left for college. I have been remiss in writing and I am very sorry for my thoughtlessness in not having written before. I will bring you up to date now, but before you read on, please sit down. You are not to read any further unless you are sitting down. Okay?

Well, then, I am getting along pretty well now. The skull fracture and concussion I got when I jumped out of the window of my dormitory when it caught fire shortly after my arrival are both pretty well healed now. I only spent two weeks in the hospital and now I can see almost normally and get those sick headaches only once a day.

Fortunately, the fire in my dormitory and my jump were witnessed by an attendant at the gas station near the dorm, and he was the one who called the fire department and the ambulance. He also visited me at the hospital, and as I had nowhere to live because of the burnt-out dormitory, he was kind enough to invite me to share his apartment with him. It's really a basement room, but it's kind of cute. He is a very fine boy and we have fallen deeply in love and are planning to get married. We haven't set the exact date yet, but it will be before my pregnancy begins to show.

Yes, Mother and Dad, I am pregnant. I know how much you are looking forward to being grandparents, and I know you will welcome the baby and give it the same love and devotion that you gave me when I was a child. The reason for the delay in our marriage is that my boyfriend has some minor infection which has prevented us from passing our pre-marital blood tests and I carelessly caught it from him. This will soon clear up with the penicillin injections I am now taking daily.

I know you will welcome him into our family with open arms. He is kind and although not well-educated, he is ambitious. Although he is of a different race and religion from us, I know your oft-expressed tolerance will not permit you to be bothered by the fact that his skin colour is somewhat darker than ours. I am sure you will love him as I do. His family background is good too, as I am told that his father is an important gun-bearer in the village in Africa from which he comes.

Now that I have brought you up to date, I want to tell you there was no dormitory fire, I did not have concussion or a skull fracture, I was not in the hospital, I am not pregnant, I am not engaged, I do not have syphilis and there is no one in my life. However I am getting a D in History and an F in Science and I wanted you to see these marks in their proper perspective.

Your loving daughter,

*Edna*

# CHAPTER 5 • LIFE

## Beyond Descartes

Since brain and memory
have long since said goodbye
'I think, therefore I am'
does not apply.

On good days, though,
I take some heart because
I think I thought
Therefore perhaps I was.
*(Martin Parker in The Spectator)*

---

## *Thoughts to get you through a crisis*

Indecision is the key to flexibility.
There is absolutely no substitute for a genuine lack of preparation.
By the time you can make ends meet, the ends have changed.
Nostalgia isn't what it used to be.
The facts, although interesting, are irrelevant.
Things are more like they are today than they have ever been before.
Everything should be made as simple as possible but no simpler.
Friends may come and go but enemies accumulate.
If you think there is some good in everybody, you haven't met everybody.
I have seen the truth and it makes no sense.

## Chinese philosophy

*Much has been written about Chinese philosophy – there is an aspect of lateral thinking about it. Here are a few examples of how it is applied by robbers in China – maybe one could develop a "Code of Conduct" for them.*

*Mind changing concept: changing the conventional way of thinking*
In a Guangzhou bank – "All don't move. Money belongs to the State, life belongs to you."
Everyone in the bank laid down quietly.

*Being professional: focus only on what you are trained to do*
One lady lay down provocatively. The robber shouted at her, "Please be civilized. This is a robbery, not a rape!"

*Experience is more importance than education*
The young robber (MBA) "Let's count how much we took!"
The old robber (primary school) "You very stupid, so much money, how to count, waste time, tonight TV news tells us how much."

*Swim with the tide: converting an unfavourable situation to your advantage*
After the robbery, the bank manager told the supervisor to call the police.
"Wait, wait, let's put the 20 million RMB we embezzled into the amount the robbers robbed."

*Happiness is most important*
The supervisor said, "It will be good if there is a robbery every month."

*Knowledge is worth as much as gold*
The day after, the TV reported 25 million stolen. The robbers were very angry and complained, "We risked our lives and only got 5 million RMB, and the bank manager got 20 million RMB with a snap of his fingers."

## LATERAL THINKING
*(solutions on next page)*

*There is a lot of discussion these days about solving problems by new mental approaches, among them lateral thinking. Here are some classical exercises better to define how this discipline works, and how to let the mind range outside the bounds of logical sequential reasoning to find surprising answers to life's many surprising questions.*

1. A man lives on the top floor of a very tall building. Every day he takes the elevator down to the ground floor to leave the building to go the work. Upon returning from work, however, he can only travel half way up in the elevator and has to walk up the rest of the way, unless it's raining. Why?

*Note: This is probably the best known and most celebrated of all lateral thinking puzzles. It is a true classic. Although many possible solutions fit the initial condition, only the canonical answer is truly satisfying.*

2. A man is wearing black. Black shoes, socks, trousers, coat, gloves and ski mask. He is walking down a back street with all the street lamps off. A black car is coming towards him with its lights off, but it manages to stop in time and avoid him. How did the driver spot the man?

*Note: This is logical rather than lateral, but it is a puzzle that can be solved by lateral thinking techniques. It is supposedly used by a well-known software as an interview question for prospective employees.*

3. A man went to a party and drank some punch. He then left early. Everyone else at the party who drank the punch subsequently died of poisoning. Why did the man not die?

4. A woman had two sons who were born on the same hour of the same day of the same year but were not twins.

5. A man walks into a bar and asks the barman for a glass of water. The barman pulls out a gun and points it at the man. The man says "Thank you!" and walks out.

Note: *This puzzle claims to be the best of the genre. It is simple in its statement, absolutely baffling and yet with a completely satisfying solution. Most people struggle to solve this one. Yet they like the answer when they hear it, or have the satisfaction of figuring it out.*

## Lateral thinking, solutions:

1. The man is very, very short and can only reach halfway up the row of the elevator buttons. However, if it is raining then he would have his umbrella with him and could press the higher buttons with it.

2. It was day time.

3. The poison in the punch came from the ice cubes. When the man drank the punch early in the party, the ice was fully frozen. Gradually it melted, poisoning the punch.

4. They were two of a set of triplets (or quadruplets, etc.)

*This puzzle stumps many people. They try outlandish solutions involving test-tube babies or surrogate mothers. Why does the brain search for complex solutions when there is a much simpler one available?*

5. The man had hiccups. The barman recognized this from his speech and drew the gun in order to give him a shock. It worked and cured the hiccups-so the man no long needed the water.

*This is a simple puzzle to state but a difficult one to solve. It is a perfect example of a seemingly irrational and incongruous situation having a simple and complete explanation. Amazingly, this classic puzzle seems to work in different cultures and languages.*

*These exercises do not measure intelligence, fluency with words, creativity, or mathematical ability. They will, however, give you some measure of your mental flexibility.*

## *The differences between full-time prison and a full-time job*

1. In prison you spend the majority of your time in an 8 ft x 10 ft cell
   At work you spend most of your time in a 6 ft x 8 ft cubicle
2. In prison you get three meals a day
   At work you only get a break for one meal and you pay for it
3. In prison you get time off for good behaviour
   At work you get rewarded with more work and more responsibility
4. In prison a guard opens and closes all doors for you
   At work you have to do it yourself.
5. In prison you can watch TV and play games
   At work you get fired for watching TV and playing games
6. In prison you get your own toilet
   At work you have to share
7. In prison all expenses are paid by taxpayers with no work required
   At work you pay expenses to go to work then get taxes deducted to pay for the prisoners
8. In prison there are warders who are sometimes sadistic
   At work there are managers who may be liable for harassment

## *"I'm My Own Grandpa"*

*This was a novelty song written by Dwight Latham and Moe Jaffe, and performed by Lonzo and Oscar in 1947. Apparently it was inspired by a Mark Twain anecdote, in which Twain proved it would be possible for a man to become his own grandfather. Through an unlikely (but legal) combination of marriages, he becomes stepfather to his own stepmother — and so, tacitly dropping the "step-" modifiers, he becomes his own grandfather."*
*Acknowledgement: The above information was found in Wikipedia*
*There are many clips of it on the Internet, one sung by Ray Stevens which shows a progressive family tree as the song goes on:*
*http://www.youtube.com/watch?v=eYlJH81dSiw.*
*(You'll have to put up with what sounds like synthetic laughter in the background...)*

Many, many years ago when I was twenty-three
I was married to a widow who was pretty as could be
This widow had a grown-up daughter who had hair of red
My father fell in love with her and soon they too were wed

This made my dad my son-in-law and really changed my life
For now my daughter was my mother, 'cos she was my father's wife
And to complicate the matter, even though it brought me joy
I soon became the father of a bouncing baby boy

My little baby then became a brother-in-law to dad
And so became my uncle, though it made me very sad
For if he were my uncle, then that also made him brother
Of the widow's grownup daughter, who was of course my step-mother

Father's wife then had a son who kept them on the run
And he became my grandchild, for he was my daughter's son
My wife is now my mother's mother and it makes me blue
Because although she is my wife, she's my grandmother too

Now if my wife is my grandmother, then I'm her grandchild
And every time I think of it, it nearly drives me wild
'Cause now I have become the strangest case you ever saw
As husband of my grandmother, I am my own grandpa

I'm my own grandpa, I'm my own grandpa
It sounds funny, I know but it really is so
I'm my own grandpa

*A French translation of this story was found in the desk of an old doctor in Switzerland. The Swiss doctor noted: "I don't know how I have brought myself to understand that. But if this story seems inconclusive, I am ready to begin again at the beginning."*

## Death

Death is nothing at all. I have only slipped away into the next room. I am I and you are you, whatever we were to each other, that we are still. Call me by my old familiar name, speak to me in the easy way you always used. Put no difference into your tone, wear no forced air of solemnity or sorrow. Laugh as we always laughed at the little jokes we enjoyed together. Pray, smile, think of me, pray for me. Let my name be the household name that it always was. Let it be spoken without effect, without a ghost of a shadow in it. Life means all that it ever meant. It is the same as it ever was, there is absolutely unbroken continuity. What is death but a negligible accident? Why should I be out of mind because I am out of sight? I am but waiting for you for an interval, somewhere very near, just around the corner … all is well.

*Henry Scott-Holland, 1847-1918, a Canon of St. Paul's Cathedral.*

## CHAPTER 6 • FINANCE

### The Bank Loan

A successful businessman walks into a bank in New York City and asks for the loan officer. He says he is going to Europe on business for two weeks for a last minute emergency and needs to borrow $5,000.

The bank officer says the bank will need some kind of security for such a loan. So the businessman hands over the keys to a new Rolls Royce parked on the street in front of the bank. Everything checks out, and the bank agrees to accept the car as collateral for the loan. An employee drives the Rolls into the bank's underground garage and parks it there.

Two weeks later, the man returns, repays the $5,000 and the interest, which comes to $15.41. The loan officer says, "We are very happy to have had your business, and this transaction has worked out very nicely, but we are little puzzled. While you were away, we checked you out and found that you are a multimillionaire. What puzzles us is why would you bother to borrow $5,000?"

The successful businessman replied, "Where else in New York can I park my car for two weeks for 15 bucks?"

### The Checking Account

Client: I want to open a f*****g checking account.

Lady:  I beg your pardon, what did you say?"

Client: Listen dammit, I said I want to open a f*****g checking account right now.

Lady:  Sir, I'm sorry but we do not tolerate that kind of language in this bank!

Client: Let me speak to your f*****g manager!

The Lady left the counter and went over to the manager and told him of her situation. They both returned to the counter.

Manager: Excuse me Sir, we do not appreciate abusive language, nor do we expect our staff to tolerate it. Now, what seems to be the problem here?

Client: There's no damn problem! I just won 50 million in the lottery and I want to open a f*****g checking account in this damn bank.

Manager: I see, Sir, and this bitch is giving you a hard time?

## *A slow day in a Greek village…*

It is a slow day in a little Greek village. The rain is beating down and the streets are deserted. Times are tough, everybody is in debt, and everybody lives on credit.

On this particular day a rich German tourist is driving through the village, stops at the local hotel and lays a €100 note on the desk; telling the hotel owner that he wants to inspect the rooms upstairs in order to pick one to spend the night.

The owner gives him some keys and as soon as the visitor has walked upstairs, grabs the €100 note and runs next door to pay his debt to the butcher.

The butcher takes the €100 note and runs down the street to repay his debt to the pig farmer.

The pig farmer takes the €100 note and heads off to pay his bill at the supplier of feed and fuel.

The guy at the Farmers' Co-op takes the €100 note and runs to pay his drink bill at the tavern.

The tavern owner slips the money along to the local prostitute drinking at the bar, who despite the hard times has had to offer him "services" on credit.

The hooker then rushes to the hotel and pays off her room bill to the hotel owner with the €100 note.

The hotel proprietor then places the €100 note back on the counter so that the rich traveller will not suspect anything. At that moment the traveller comes down the stairs, picks up the €100 note, states that the rooms are not satisfactory, pockets the money, and leaves town.

No one has produced anything. No one has earned anything. However, the whole village is now out of debt and looking to the future with a lot more optimism.

And that, Ladies and Gentlemen, is how the bailout package works!

## Letter to a Bank

Dear Sirs,

In view of what seems to be happening internationally with banks at the moment, I was wondering if you could advise me. One of my cheques has been returned marked "Insufficient funds." Could you please tell me if that refers to me or to you. Many thanks.

Yours truly,

*M.J.C.*


Dear M.J.C.

Thank you for your letter of 20th inst.

You are incorrect in your assumption that your cheque was returned due to there being insufficient funds in your own account. Indeed I can confirm that your current balance is more than sufficient to cover the amount. Unfortunately, when we tried to send this money to the payee bank via Bankers Automated Clearing Services (BACS), it was returned to us marked "Insufficient funds available." Upon investigation, we see that we have a little problem with our own liquidity position.

Please be assured that this is only temporary and that it is being sorted out. Indeed, we have actually decided to sell a few shares to the government to raise a little more cash although this has meant that we have had to say a fond farewell to both our highly respected CEO and our Chairman whom I think you know well. Nevertheless, may I respectfully suggest that you re-present the cheque in about six weeks time when we hope to have sufficient funds available.

Please be assured that we are still able to take your deposits. In the event we should mislay these or make an unwise investment, the government in its infinite wisdom has decided to guarantee these up to a limit of £50,000.

Please forgive the tardy reply to your letter, but it was unfortunately sent to the chief cashier who appears to have gone on a rather extended holiday. We remain your obedient servant

Yours truly,

*C.H.W.*

# CHAPTER 7 • GOLF

### *Ode to golf*

IN MY HAND I HOLD A BALL,
WHITE AND DIMPLED, RATHER SMALL,
OH, HOW BLAND IT DOES APPEAR,
THIS HARMLESS LOOKING LITTLE SPHERE.

BY IT'S SIZE I COULD NOT GUESS,
THE AWESOME STRENGTH IT DOES POSSESS.
BUT SINCE I FELL BENEATH ITS SPELL,
I'VE WANDERED THROUGH THE FIRES OF HELL.

MY LIFE HAS NOT BEEN QUITE THE SAME,
SINCE I CHOSE TO PLAY THIS STUPID GAME.
IT RULES MY MIND FOR HOURS ON END,
A FORTUNE IT HAS MADE ME SPEND.

IT'S MADE ME YELL AND CURSE AND CRY,
I HATE MYSELF AND WANT TO DIE.

IT PROMISES A THING CALLED PAR,
IF I CAN HIT IT STRAIGHT AND FAR.
TO MASTER SUCH A TINY BALL,
SHOULD NOT BE VERY HARD AT ALL.
BUT MY DESIRES THE BALL REFUSES,
AND DOES EXACTLY AS IT CHOOSES.

## *Learning to Play*

"Darling," my wife said to me one day "It's time you learnt to play golf. You know, the game where you chase a ball all over the country when you're too old to chase women."

So I went to see Jones and asked if he could teach me how to play. He said, "Sure, you got balls, haven't you?"

I said, "Yes, but sometimes on cold mornings, they're kind of hard to find."

"Bring them to the clubhouse tomorrow," he continued, "and we'll tee off." "What's tee off?" I asked. "It's a golf term. We tee off in front of the club house."

"Not for me," I replied. "You can tee off there if you want to, but I'll tee off behind the barn somewhere."

"No, no," he said. "A tee is a little thing about the size of your little finger." "Yeah, I got one of those."

"Well," he said, "you stick it in the ground and put your ball on top of it."

I asked, "So, you play golf sitting down? I always thought that you stood up and walked around."

"You do," he said. "You are standing up when you put your ball on the tee." Well folks, I thought that was stretching things a little bit too far and I said so.

Next he said, "You've got a bag, haven't you?"

"Sure," I said.

"Well," he said. "Can you open your bag and take one out?"

"I suppose I could," I replied. "But damned if I'm going to."

He asked me if I didn't have a zipper on my bag, but I told him I had the old-fashioned type. Then he asked me if I knew how to hold my club. Well, after fifty years, I should have some sort of idea and told him so.

He said, "You take your club in both hands." I knew right then he didn't know what he was talking about.

"Then," he said. "You swing it over your shoulder."

"No, no, that's not me, you're talking about my brother."

He asked me "How do you hold your club?" And without thinking, I answered, "With two fingers."

He said that was not right and got behind me and put both arms around me and told me to bend over and he would show me how. He couldn't catch me there because I didn't spend four years in the Navy for nothing.

He said, "You hit the ball with your club and it will soar and soar." I said "I bet it would."

Then he said, "and when you are on the green …."

"What's the green?" I asked. "That's where the hole is." he answered. "Sure you're not colour-blind?" I asked.

"No…, then you take your putter…."

"What's the putter?" I asked.

"That's the smallest club."

"That's what I've got, a putter."

"You put the ball in the hole."

"You mean the putter?"

"No, the putter is too big for that."

"Well, I've seen holes big enough to take a horse and cart! What happens then?"

"You go on to the next seventeen holes."

"You're not talking to me, after two holes I'm shot to hell."

"Well that's the end and the flag goes back in the hole."

My, what a game!!!

# A PSALM FOR A SABBATH MORNING

The Pro is my Shepherd
I shall not slice.
He maketh me to Drive Straight
Down Green Fairways,
He leadeth me in the Paths of Accuracy
For my Games Sake.
Yea, though I clip through the Roughs
In the Shadow of Sand Traps,
I will fear No Bogies.
For his advice is with me,
His Putter and Irons
They comfort me.
He prepareth a Strategy for me
In the presence of mine Opponents,
He appointeth my head with Confidence:
The Cup will not be runneth over!
Surely Birdies and Eagles shall follow me
All the rounds of my Life.

And I will score in the Low Eighties—
Forever

## *Professional Caddies*

*Some people think that golf caddies are just bag carriers (some are). Others are just ball watchers, but the real golf caddies have a golfing life of their own. Here are some examples of the latter:*

Golfer: Think I'm going to drown myself in the lake.
Caddie: Think you can keep your head down that long?

Golfer: I'd move heaven and earth to break 100 on this course!
Caddie: Try heaven. You've already moved most of the earth.

Golfer: Do you think my game is improving?
Caddie: Yes sir, you miss the ball much closer now.

Golfer: Do you think I can get there with a 5 iron?
Caddie: Eventually.

Golfer: You've got to be the worst caddy in the world.
Caddie: I don't think so. That would be too much of a coincidence.

Golfer: Please stop checking your watch all the time. It's a real distraction.
Caddie: It's not a watch. It's a compass.

Golfer: How do you like my game?
Caddie: Very good, sir, but personally I prefer golf.

Golfer: Do you think it's a sin to play on Sunday.
Caddie: (sotto voce) The way you play it's a sin any day.

Golfer: This is the worst course I've ever played on.
Caddie: This isn't the golf course. We left that twenty minutes ago.

Golfer: That can't be my ball, it's too old.
Caddie: It's been a long time since we teed off, sir.

## The widow

John decided to go golfing in Scotland with his buddy, Keith. So they loaded up John's mini-van and headed north. After driving for a few hours, they got caught in a terrible blizzard. They pulled into a nearby farm and asked the attractive lady who answered the door if they could spend the night.

"I realize it's terrible weather out there and I have this huge house all to myself, but I'm recently widowed," she explained, "and I'm afraid the neighbours will talk if I let you stay in my house."

"Don't worry," John said. "We'll be happy to sleep in the barn. And if the weather breaks, we'll be gone at first light."

The lady agreed, and the two men found their way to the barn and settled in for the night.

Come morning, the weather had cleared, and they got on their way. They enjoyed a great weekend of golf.

But about nine months later, John got an unexpected letter from an attorney. It took him a few minutes to figure it out, but he finally determined that it was from the attorney of that attractive widow he had met on the golf weekend.

He dropped in on his friend Keith and asked, "Keith, do you remember that good-looking widow from the farm we stayed at on our golf holiday in Scotland about 9 months ago?"

'Yes, I do," Keith replied.

"Did you, er, happen to get up in the middle of the night, go up to the house and pay her a visit?"

"Well, um, yes," Keith said ,a little embarrassed about being found out. "I have to admit that I did."

"And did you happen to give her my name instead of telling her your name?"

Keith's face turned beet red and he said, "Yeah, look, I'm sorry, buddy. I'm afraid I did. But why do you ask?"

"Well, she just died and left me everything!"

## *Tom and Bill*

There were two men on the first tee.
"I'm alone. If you are too, why don't we play together. My name's Tom."
"Sure. I'd like that. I'm Bill."
There were two women playing very slowly in front of them.
"Tom, shall I ask if they'll let us pass?"
When he was thirty yards away, he turned round and came back
"I can't. One of them's my wife and the other my mistress."
"OK Bill, I'll go." When he came back: "I couldn't ask either..."

*Not a particularly good joke as told to me, or maybe a true story. But what about when, as almost certainly, they met up in the clubhouse.*
*1. Would the men have revealed all to their wives? I'm sure not.*
*2. If it had been the women, I'm sure they would have asked to pass.*
*3. The men would have kept it quiet.*
*4. The women would have had questions.*

*And I would have loved to have been at the table at dinner with the four of them afterwards!*

## *Around the Course in Par*

A man, his son and grandson were waiting to tee off when a very attractive lady walked up and said, "The Secretary told me you might be interested in my making up a four-ball." The three of them gave three different generational answers but all were positive.

She said, "I play off a five handicap but my real ambition is to go round this course in par. It would mean a lot to me."

In due course they reached the eighteenth green and her ball was on the green but there was a double break between it and the hole making it a very difficult putt for par to achieve her ambition. She repeated, "This means a lot to me. Whoever can help me achieve my ambition, I'll pay for a champagne dinner and spend the whole evening with him."

The grandson jumped up saying, "No problem. Just putt to the top of the first break and it will run down into the hole."

"No, no!", argued his father, "it'll get too much speed. You must putt gently in the space between the two breaks and a straight putt will take it into the hole."

The grandfather picked up her ball and held it out to her saying, "It's a gimme."

She took the ball with a smile and said, "Your place or mine?"

# CHAPTER 8 • RELIGION

## *The Jew and the Italian*

Several centuries ago, the Pope decreed all Jews had to convert to Catholicism or leave Italy. There was a huge outcry from the Jewish community, so the Pope offered a deal.

He would have a religious debate with the leader of the Jewish Community. If the Jews won, they could stay in Italy; if the Pope won they would have to convert or leave. The Jewish people met and selected an aged and wise rabbi to represent them in the debate. However as the Rabbi spoke no Italian and the Pope spoke no Yiddish, they agreed that it would be a "silent" debate.

On the chosen day the Pope and the Rabbi sat opposite each other. The Pope raised his hand and showed three fingers. The Rabbi looked back and raised one finger.

Next, the Pope waved his finger around his head. The Rabbi pointed to the ground where he sat.

The Pope brought out the Communion wafer and a chalice of wine. The rabbi pulled out an apple.

With that the Pope stood up and declared that he was beaten, and that the Rabbi was too clever. The Jews could stay in Italy. Later the Cardinals met with the Pope and asked him what had happened. The Pope explained, "First I held up three fingers to represent the Trinity. He responded by holding up one finger to remind me that there is only one God common to both our beliefs.

"Then I waved my finger around my head to show him that God was all around us. He responded by pointing to the ground to show that God was also right here with us.

"I pulled out the wine and wafer, to show that God absolves us of all our sins. He pulled out an apple to remind me of the original sin. He had me beaten at every move and so I lost."

Meanwhile the Jewish community gathered to ask the Rabbi how he had won. "I haven't a clue," answered the Rabbi. "First he said to me that we had three days to get out of Italy, so I gave him the finger. Then he tells me that the whole country must be cleared of Jews and I said to him that we were staying right here."

"And then what?" a woman asked. "Who knows?" the Rabbi answered. "He took out his lunch, so I took out mine."

## A story about Moses

An Israeli diplomat recently raised a laugh among the diplomatic community at the United Nations:

The Israeli representative declared, "Before beginning my speech, I would like to tell you a story about Moses. When he struck the rock and the water began to gush, Moses thought, "What a great opportunity to take a bath!." He undressed, carefully put his clothes on a rock and entered the water.

When he came out, his clothes were gone, stolen by a Palestinian."

The Palestinian representative, shocked and angry interrupted the speech of the representative of Israel, exclaiming, "What are you talking about? The Palestinians were not there at that time." The Israeli representative smiled and said, "Now that this is clear, I can begin my speech."

## The Jew and the Czech

A Jew and a Czech were walking in the woods. Two bears jumped and one caught the Czech and swallowed him .

The Jew escaped and called people for help. The helpers came and asked "Which one caught the Czech? The male or the female?"

The Jew replied, "The male."

But in fact it was the female.

Moral of the story: Never believe a Jew when he tells you the cheque is in the mail!

*(I must add that I read this out as a warning to my future son-in-law at my daughter's wedding, ... and it was well-received !*

## *Misprinted Church Messages*

(taken directly from church bulletins)

Wednesday the ladies liturgy society will meet. Mrs. Johnson will sing, "Put me in my little bed", accompanied by the Pastor.

Thursday at 5 pm there will be a meeting of the Little Mothers' Club. All ladies wishing to be little mothers please meet with the Pastor in his study.

The service will close with "Little Drops of Water." One of the ladies will start quietly and the rest of the congregation will join in

The ladies of the Church have cast off clothing of every kind and they may be seen in the Church basement on Friday afternoon

A Bean Supper will be held on Saturday evening in the basement. Music will follow.

Tonight's sermon: What is Hell? Come early and listen to our choir practice.

For those of you who have children and don't know it, we have a nursery downstairs.

Remember in prayer the many who are sick in our church and community.

Potluck supper: prayer and medication to follow.

Don't let worry kill you -- let the church help.

## Eve

*From the commentary on Genesis of LEVI, a third century Palestinian sage and teacher:*

When God decided to create Eve, He considered from what part of Adam to create her. Said the Almighty: "I will not use the head, lest she become conceited. I will not use the eyes, lest she be curious; nor the ear, lest she become an eavesdropper; nor the tongue, lest she be a gossip. I will not use the heart, lest she be jealous, nor the hand, lest she be grasping, nor the foot, lest she be a gadabout. I shall make her from a hidden part of man, so that even when she is naked it cannot be seen. So God created Eve from one of Adam's ribs."

*I have come across a comment by a 19th century bible student (who shall remain anonymous):"Alas, all the precautions were in vain. Woman is conceited, curious, a gossip, a chatterbox, she is jealous, grasping and a gadabout."*

## Attitude

A Jewish man was riding on the subway reading a Neo-Nazi newspaper. A friend of his who happened to be riding in the same subway car, noticed this strange phenomenon. Very upset he approached the newspaper reader "Have you lost your mind? Why are you reading a Neo-Nazi newspaper?"

The man replied, "I used to read the Jewish newspaper, but what did I find? Anti-Semitism in Europe, terrorism in Israel, Jews disappearing through assimilation and marriage, Jews living in poverty. So I switched to the Neo-Nazi newspaper. Now what do I find? Jews own all the banks, Jews control the media. Jews are all rich and powerful, Jews rule the world. The news is so much better."

## Back to Front

On a train, a Rabbi was sitting opposite a priest, looking at him curiously.

The Priest: "Excuse me, you are looking at me as if there is something wrong."

The Rabbi: "No, I must apologise, but I see that when you dressed this morning, you put on your collar back to front."

The Priest: "Ah, that is not a mistake, it shows I'm a priest.

The Rabbi: "Yes, but I am a priest as well."

The Priest: "No, I am a Father."

The Rabbi: "I am a father as well. At home, I have three little………

The Priest: "I am afraid you still don't understand, I am a Father of thousands."

The Rabbi: "Oh, so maybe then it's not your collar, but your trousers, that should be back to front."

## Naming the Ranch

Two Texans are sitting on a plane from Dallas with a little old Jewish Texan between them.

One said, "My name is Roger, I own 250,000 acres and a thousand head of cattle. The ranch is called The Jolly Roger."

The second one said, "My name is John. I own 350,000 acres and have five thousand head of cattle. My ranch is called Big John's."

"What about you?" they both asked. "My name is Irving and I own only 300 acres." "What do you raise?" "Nothing."

What do you call your ranch then?"

"Downtown Dallas!"

## A Seat that Suits

During the last holiday season, many individuals expressed concern over the seating arrangements in the synagogue. In order for us to place you in a seat which will best suit you, we ask you to complete the following questionnaire and return it to the synagogue office as soon as possible.

1. I wish to be placed in a seat next to someone who would like to discuss the following topics:

--- the stock market    --- my neighbours

--- sports    --- my relatives

--- fashion news    --- the Rabbi

--- general gossip    --- the Cantor

--- specific gossip    --- the gabbay

Specify _____

2. I wish to be seated where:

--- I can see my spouse

--- I cannot see my spouse

--- I can see my friend's spouse

--- My spouse cannot see me seeing my friend's spouse

--- No one on the bimah can see me talking during services

--- I can sleep during services

--- I can sleep during the Rabbi's sermon (extra charge).

3. I wish to be located next to the following so that I can get free professional advice (please underline):

Doctor – Dentist – Nutritionist – Psychiatrist – Podriatrist – Chiropracter – Stockbroker – Accountant – Lawyer – Real estate agent – Sexologist (waiting list) – golf pro (extra charge)

4.     I want a seat located (circle one):

Near the exit – near the bathroom – near my in-laws – far from my in-laws – far from my ex-in-laws – near available women – near single men

## Neighbours – The Last Two Jews in Kabul

*by Paul Holmes of Reuters in Kabul*

*I have just finished reading* The Little Coffee House in Kabul, *first published in 2011, which mentions a meeting with the last Jew in Kabul, Zebolan Simanto, then in bad shape and living a miserable life with no income and relying on visitors to live.*

From the Financial Times, Monday, 3rd December 2001

Yitzhak Levy and Zebolan Simanto say they are the last two Jews in Afghanistan and they hate each other with a vengeance. "Yitzhak and the Taliban, they're the same," Mr. Simanto, 41, said, pressing the tips of two fingers together to make the point.

Across the courtyard of a crumbling apartment on Flower Street that used to be home to some thirty Jewish families, Mr. Levy is just as bitter about his neighbour. The building has no glass in its windows, no running water and two synagogues, one that Mr. Simanto climbs into through a window, and one which Mr. Levy keeps under lock and key.

"All my problems are because of Zebolan," said Mr. Levy, a squat man with a flowing white beard and battered sheepskin Astrakhan hat, who gave his age as 60. He recites a litany of woes, capped by accusations that the only other Jew in Kabul had denounced him to the Taliban as a spy for Israel and landed him in jail five times. Mr. Levy, a traditional healer born in the western city of Herat, remained in Kabul when the Taliban took over in 1996. Mr. Simanto, a dealer in carpets, also from Herat, spent six years travelling in Israel, Uzbekistan and Turkmenistan. He returned to Kabul in 1998. Both say their wives are in Israel.

Muslim neighbours regard the pair with a mixture of affection and amusement. At night, they say they can hear them shout, hurling abuse and charges of treachery and immorality at each other like some unhappy couple imprisoned in a marriage gone sour.

### Stand or Sit?

During a service at an old synagogue in Eastern Europe, when the Shema prayer was being recited, half the congregants stood up and half remained sitting. The half that was sitting started yelling at the half that were standing and vice-versa. The Rabbi, learned as he was, did not know what to do. His congregation suggested he consult a house-bound 98-year-old man who was one of the original members of the synagogue. So the Rabbi took a member of each faction with him to see the old man.

The one whose followers stood during the prayer asked whether it was the tradition to stand during the prayer. "No, that is not the tradition," was the answer. With a satisfied smile the other representative said,

"So it is the tradition to sit during the prayer." "No," replied the old man. "That is not the tradition."

The Rabbi intervened saying, "But the congregants fight all the time, yelling at each other about whether they should sit or stand."

The old man interrupted, exclaiming, "*THAT* is the tradition!"

## What not to call your dog

Everybody that has a dog calls him Rover or Boy. I called mine Sex. Now Sex has been very embarrassing for me. When I went to the City Hall to renew his licence, I told the clerk that I would like to have a license for Sex. He said, "I'd like to have one too." "No," I told him, "You don't understand. I've had Sex since I was nine years old.." He looked at me and said "You must have been quite a kid!"

When I got married and went on honeymoon, I took the dog with me. I told the hotel clerk that I wanted a room for my wife and myself and a small room for Sex. He said that every room in the place was for sex. "No," I said, "You don't under-stand. Sex keeps me awake at night." "Me too," he said.

After my wife and I separated, I entered Sex for a contest, but before the competition began, the dog ran away. Another contestant asked me why I was just standing there looking around. I told him I had planned to have Sex in the contest. He told me I should have sold my own tickets. "But you don't understand," I said, "I was planning to have Sex on TV." He called me a show-off.

When we separated, we went to court to fight for custody of the dog. I told the judge, "Your Honour, I had Sex long before we were married. "Me too," the Judge said. Then I told him that once I was married, Sex left me." "Me too," he said again.

Last night Sex ran off again. I spent hours looking around town for him. A cop came over to me and asked "What are you doing in this alley at 4 o'clock in the morning?" "I'm looking for Sex." I answered. My case comes up on Friday.

### The Hazards of Abbreviation

*I read the next one out at my son's school-leaving dinner at Harrow and got the biggest laugh of the evening*

A young married couple had been shown around a house which there were proposing to purchase by the local vicar, who was deputising for the local estate agent. When they returned home they realised that they had not been shown the W.C. So they wrote to the vicar.

The vicar thought they were referring to the Wesleyan Chapel, and replied thus:

"The W.C. is about three miles away, but nobody minds as they only go on alternate weeks. Seats are provided, but most people stand and sing. Children are attended to separately. The man in charge is excellent and attends to everyone's needs. Printed sheets are provided, but should be returned afterwards as they are used again next time."

## Words and sounds

*Here is a great example of how words and sounds, i.e. double meanings, can be used to great effect:*

> She offered her honour,
>
> He honoured her offer,
>
> **And so all night long**
>
> **It was on'er and off'er**

## WHAT IS IT?

This useful tool, commonly found in the range of 6 inches long, and the functioning of which is enjoyed by numbers of both sexes, is usually found hung, dangling loosely. Ready for instant action, it boasts a clump of little hairy things at one end and a small hole at the other. In use, it is inserted, almost always willingly, sometimes slowly, sometimes quickly, into a warm, fleshy, moist opening where it is thrust in and drawn out again and again many times in succession, often quickly and accompanied by squirming bodily movements. Anyone found listening in will mot surely recognize the rhythmic, pulsing sounds resulting from the well-lubricated movements.

When finally withdrawn, it leaves behind a juicy, frothy, sticky white substance, some of which will need cleaning from the other surfaces of the opening and some from its long glistening shaft. After everything is done and the flowing and cleansing liquids have ceased emanating, it is returned to its freely hanging state of rest, ready for another bit of action, hopefully reaching its bristling climax twice or three times a day, but often much less.

As you have already no doubt guessed, the answer to this riddle is none other than … your very own toothbrush.

## Little David

Little David was in his 4th grade class when the teacher asked the children what their fathers did for a living. All the typical answers came up: fireman, policeman, salesman, doctor, lawyer, etc.

David was being uncharacteristically quiet, so the teacher asked him about his father.

"My father's an exotic dancer in a gay cabaret and takes off all his clothes in front of other men and they put money in his underwear. Sometimes, if the offer is really good, he will go home with some guy and make love with him for money."

The teacher, obviously shaken by this statement, hurriedly set the other children to work on some exercises and took little David aside to ask him, "Is that really true about your father?" "No," replied David, "He works for the Republican National Committee to re-elect George Bush, but I was too embarrassed to say that in front of the other kids."

## A Matter of Choice

A man came home after a heavy day in the office and was greeted by his wife in a shimmering transparent nightdress.

"Tie me up," she purred, "and you can do anything you like."

So he tied her up and went golfing.

## Communication

A judge was interviewing a woman regarding her pending divorce, and asked, "What are the grounds for your divorce?""

She replied, "About four acres and a nice little home in the middle of the property with a stream running by."

"No," he said. "I mean, what is the foundation of this case?"

"It is made of concrete, brick and mortar," she responded.

"I mean," continued the judge, "What are your relations like?"

"I have an aunt and uncle living here in town, and so do my husband's parents."

He asked, "Do you have a real grudge?"

"No," she replied. "We have a two-car carport and have never really needed one."

"Please," he tried again. "Is there any infidelity in your marriage?"

"Yes, both my son and daughter have stereo sets. We don't necessarily like the music, but the answer to your question is yes."

"Ma'am, does your husband ever beat you up?"

"Yes," she responded. "About twice a week he gets up earlier than I do."

Finally, in frustration, the judge asked, "Lady, why do you want a divorce?"

"Oh, I don't want a divorce," she replied. "I've never wanted a divorce. My husband does. He says he can't communicate with me."

## A Matter of Perspective

Two Irishmen were sitting in a pub having beer and watching the brothel across the street. Seeing the local Baptist minister walk into the brothel, one of them said, "Aye, 'tis a shame to see a man of the cloth goin' bad."

A bit later, they saw the rabbi enter the brothel, and the other Irishman shook his head sadly and said. "Aye, 'tis a shame to see that the Jews are fallin' victim to temptation."

It wasn't much later that they saw the Catholic priest enter the brothel. They were silent for a few minutes. Then, one of the Irishmen sighed and said, "Sure and 'tis a great pity to see such a thing. One of those poor girls must be quite ill!"

## Sex Therapy

A couple were consulting a sex therapist in his surgery. After the usual formalities, the man says, "Will you watch us have sexual intercourse?"

The doctor raises both eyebrows, but he is so amazed that such a couple is asking for sexual advice that he agrees. When the couple finishes, the doctor says, "There's absolutely nothing wrong with the way you have intercourse." He thanks them for coming, wishes them good luck, charges them $50 and says goodbye.

The next week, the same couple returns and asks the sex therapist to watch again. The sex therapist is a bit puzzled, but agrees. This happens several weeks in a row. The couple makes an appointment, has intercourse with no problems, pays the doctor, then leaves.

Finally, after three months of this routine, the doctor says, "I'm sorry, but I have to ask. Just what are you trying to find out?"

"We're not trying to find out anything," the man answered, "She's married, so we can't go to her house."

"And I'm married, so we can't go to my house," adds the woman, "The Holiday Inn charges $98, the Hilton charges $139. We can do it here for $50, and I get $43 back from Medicare insurance.

## Dental Expertise

A guy and a girl meet in a bar, they get to talking, he mentions that he is a dentist so one thing leads to another and they go back to her place and have sex. Exhausted after a great session of bodily enjoyment the dentist falls back and lights up a cigarette.

"That was great," he sighed.

"Yeah, you must be a great dentist," the lady answered.

"Why do you say that?"

"I didn't feel a thing..."

## A Christmas Wish

**A small boy wrote to
Santa Claus:**

**Dear Santa,
Please send me a baby brother.**

**Santa wrote back:**

**'Send me your mother...'**

## A Marriage that Worked

*There are many definitions of a perfect marriage. I see this as an attempt to give an objective appraisal of two subjective situations. The definition that I propose is: "one that works."*

One evening, an elderly man said to his wife, "We are about to celebrate our 60th wedding anniversary. We've had a good life together, full of successes and disappointments, with problems to be solved and blessings to rejoice in. But there's something I've always wondered about. Tell me the truth. Have you ever been unfaithful to me?"

She hesitated a moment and then said, "Yes, three times."

"Three times?" in shock, "How could that happen?"

"Well, do you remember right after we were married, and we were so broke that the bank was about to close on our little house?"

"Yes, of course I remember. Those were really rough times."

"And remember when I went to see the banker one night and the next day the banker extended our loan?"

"Gosh, that's not easy for me to accept, but I guess it solved a problem for our marriage. I guess I must forgive you ... But what was the next time?"

"Well, do you remember, years later when you almost died from that heart problem because we couldn't afford an operation?"

"Yes of course." said Sydney.

"Then you will remember that right after that I went to see the doctor, and he performed the operation at no cost?"

"Yes, I remember," answered Sydney, "and as much as that shocks me, I do understand that you did what you did out of love for me, so I forgive you. So, what was the third time?"

Marsha lowered her head and said, "Do you remember when you ran for president of your golf club and you needed 26 more votes?"

# CHAPTER 10 • FAMILY STORIES

## *My mother writes:*

An early family story dates from 1928, when my father, later Wing Commander Edward (Teddy ) Smouha was at Magdalene College Cambridge, in his third and final year and had just been selected to run in the 1928 Olympic games for Great Britain, where he finally ended up winning a Bronze Medal in the 4 x 100 metre relay. He was obviously known even outside University circles.

One day he was in his rooms when the porter knocked on his door. He came in and said, "I don't know what you've been up to, sir, but there are two policemen who want to speak to you."

"Well, show them in," replied Teddy. After greetings had been exchanged, they said, "We heard you are a good runner, so we wanted to ask if you would do something for us. Some undergraduates have been taking helmets off our men's heads and running off with them. We think it is a sort of game. The other day when the Inspector was here he asked how it could have happened. One of our officers spoke up and said the policemen must have sold them. So, sir, we want to ask you to take that officer's helmet."

"How could I do that?" Teddy asked. (My mother has not written a detail I remember of this story: that the helmets were secured by a strap under the chin so that the only way to take one off was by lifting it off from the back; my father practised this using other hats the evening before acceding to the policemen's request.)

"Well, tomorrow evening at 7 o'clock he will be on his beat on Chesterton Road, so if you could take it off him then you would be doing our company a great service." So Teddy accepted to do it.

The next evening he put on his gym shoes and went to Chesterton Road, where he saw the officer striding along. So he ran up behind him, flipped the helmet from the back of his head and it flew off. He caught it and ran as fast as he could to his rooms and hid it under his bed.

A few days later, the same two policemen came and thanked him, and told him that the officer had asked to be removed to another company because he was so ashamed. "Where is the helmet?" they asked. Teddy fetched it and they produced a hammer and nails and hung it on the wall.

Some five years later, we visited Cambridge, taking our baby, Dicky, with us. As we walked along with the pram, a policeman on the other side of the road called out and came across and had a chat and joked with us. That helmet went with us to Egypt, where, unfortunately, it has remained with our other confiscated belongings.

## The Air Marshal and the Lion

*During World War II, my father, as CO of Air Booking Centre covering all air transport in and out of the Middle East, came across many spectacular stories, most of which he could not tell. The following story was one of my mother's favourites and this is how she told it:*

There was a RAF staging post in the Sudan consisting of a few huts where air traffic flying between Cairo and South Africa broke their journey.

One morning, a corporal saw something in a corner outside one of the huts and found that it was a newborn baby lion abandoned by its mother. He took it inside and it grew up there as a pet. They made a cage for him behind the huts, where he was to sleep at night, but he was allowed to wander as he wanted all day. He soon grew up to be a full-sized lion.

Whenever he heard an aeroplane approaching, he went near to where it would be landing, and as soon as the door was opened, he jumped inside to welcome the crew, then went out and waited until the plane took off.

One day an Air Marshal broke his journey there. When in the Mess, he told the company that in future the lion must be shut in its cage whenever an aeroplane was expected, as it would be very frightening for anyone passing through to find themselves face to face with a lion. "And if," he continued, "I hear it has not been shut up, I shall shoot it!" So not wanting to lose what had become a member of the outpost, the lion was always shut up in its cage whenever an aircraft was expected.

The Air Marshal came through some time later and strode into the Mess shouting that he had given an order which had not been obeyed – the lion was out as before. "I gave it a great kick in its chest and shouted, 'GET OUT OF HERE!' He growled and growled, turned round and went off into the bush. Why, what is the matter with you all?"

There was a brief silence and then someone spoke. "Our lion has been in his cage all morning. The one you kicked was a wild one from the bush!"

They were all struck dumb – especially the Air Marshal.

## The Banana Story

*(also as told by my mother)*

In the last two-and-a-half years of WW1, Teddy set up and commanded his own unit as part of Transport Command. It was called the Air Booking Centre and coordinated all non-operational aircraft carrying war equipment and personnel in and out off the Middle East, through a series of representatives in the various aerodromes and his central office in downtown Cairo, which had some seventy officers, airmen and women.

One day a sergeant came into his office and said there were two ladies from the Red Cross wanting to speak to him, so he had them shown in. They told Teddy that they had been contacted by the Red Cross in England about the baby daughter of a seaman in the Merchant Navy. The baby was seriously ill, and the doctor had said that if they could get some bananas from abroad, as they were among certain foods completely unobtainable in England (I remember this as a big problem), and that eating them could save the baby's life (potassium?). So could he arrange for some bananas to be sent?

He answered, "I could do this, but you must not mention it to anyone when you leave this room, as if it were known, I could be in a lot of trouble.; but I will get some bananas and all you have to do is get me the name and address of the baby's home." The ladies were very grateful and promised not to say a word to anyone.

So Teddy sent an airman out to buy two huge bunches of bananas just as they were cut off the tree, and made arrangements for them to be flown out that night. They were delivered next morning by an RAF staff car.

A few days later, Teddy's senior officer, an Air Vice Marshal, telephoned him in his office and asked him to come and see him in Middle East Headquarters. When he arrived there and was shown to the AVM's office, the AVM held up the previous day's Daily Mirror the front page of which carried a heading, RAF sends bananas from Egypt to save baby's life. "Do you know anything about this?" he asked. "Yes, I sent them," Teddy replied, "I thought of the father of the baby away at sea, worrying about his child and how glad he would be to know that she was being cared for." "Well," said the AVM "If this comes up in London, I can't do anything for

you." "I realise that," replied Teddy, "but if I am courtmartialled I shall have the satisfaction of knowing that I did a good job during my service in the RAF, when I return to civilian life."

He never heard any more about the incident until about 18 to 20 years later when our grandchildren's Nanny, who had looked after our children during the war, produced a recent copy of the Daily Mirror. On the front page was a photo of a hospital nurse of the RAF being decorated or given a diploma. The officer doing the presentation asked her why she had chosen that profession, and she answered, "When I was a baby someone in the RAF sent me bananas from Egypt which saved my life, so I felt I should do something to benefit other people." It was so good to have this news.

Another war story concerning my father -- this one, I believe has been handed down verbally but I think there is only one version. The date is difficult to find but it must have been a period when things were going badly for the Allies and it was before the start-up of his unit, the Air Booking Centre. This would place it around the end of 1942 when he was either a senior Flight Lieutenant or a junior Squadron Leader. For reasons we will never know MEHQ had run out of money to pay the salaries in Cairo. Furthermore there were no aircraft or ground transport available to get the money from Jerusalem where apparently the central bank accounts for the Middle East were held.

So my father was given a mission, extremely short term. "Here is a jeep and an RAF corporal driver. You are to leave within the hour, drive across Sinai to Jerusalem. You will pick up gold bars from Barclays Bank. Here is a map, drive straight back to Cairo and deposit them with Barclays Bank Cairo or with the Manager. This is his address.

"It would seem that he had a trouble-free ride to Jerusalem along a desert road which today would be called a track. Apart from a few villages every forty or so miles, the only thing they came across were some desert animals and Bedouin walking along the track. *(Where were they coming from and where were they going were the questions that we always used to put to ourselves rhetorically years later ---  no answer).* They reached Jerusalem where the gold was waiting for them and loaded the sterling five million pounds worth of gold under the seats of the open Jeep and headed back to Cairo. It seemed like an easy if exhausting mission until Until, some way along the track, they ran out of petrol (how or why, I was never told). They had just passed through one of the few villages that had a petrol pump but they knew, especially as it was getting late in the day, that there would be no further traffic until at least the next day. So he sent the Corporal to walk back to the village with a small petrol can, knowing it would be several hours before he would get back. So there he was in the middle of the desert sitting in the driver's seat of an open-sided jeep on top of five million pounds of gold with his service pistol across his knees. He told me of all the thoughts that went through his mind during those hours and what he would do and how he would react under all the different possible circumstances.

Fortunately nothing happened, so belatedly, they carried on with their journey.

They arrived in Cairo around three in the morning, exhausted. They drew up in front of the bank manager's house and my father rang at the bell several times. Finally a window opened and a man stuck out his head and said, "What the hell do you think you are doing? It's three o'clock in the morning."

"I have just come from Jerusalem with the expected delivery."

"You're late. The Bank opens at nine. Bring it round then and I'll take delivery, but not before."

"Listen, we've spent the last twenty-four hours driving through the desert and I'm going home to have a bath and bed. We are unloading the gold. I was told to deliver it directly to you. You will find it on your doorstep with the receipt you are supposed to sign. I am prepared to wait five minutes and then I'm off."

The Manager, furious, came down, signed the receipt, and they never spoke to each other again.

# CHAPTER 11 •
# CARAVANNING HOLIDAYS

My parents discovered caravanning in 1947, with a grand tour of post-war France (and continued to enjoy it in Scotland and Ireland until the late 1980s).

On our first real experience in 1947, we were two families of five, in two caravans, both towed by Bentleys, a sight for sore eyes in a war-torn countryside. Both families consisted of a couple, two sons and one daughter. But the similarity ended there. While our family was all Jewish, the other father was a very laid back Scottish Presbyterian married to a very vocal pleasantly aggressive Irish Roman Catholic, both of whom were fortunately endowed with a massive sense of humour. As soon as Ranald the Scot saw that we had finished our morning prayers, he would wander across for breakfast to escape from the clutches of his own family's morning prayers. Our travel system and daily programme were simple in what was, still that year, on deserted touristless roads: at lunch we would consult our pre-war Guide Michelin near where we would be landing. We would drive directly to the best restaurant and pass on to Step B.

Step B: "We are ten people who wish to dine in your restaurant tonight." "We are most happy."

"Yes but there is a condition that you are well placed to solve. We need to find the perfect beauty spot to park our caravans."

"That is no problem!" And we had some wonderful places, the corner of a field, on a lake, by a river.

From then on, this became a holiday way of life for my parents but thereafter only in Scotland and Ireland, the next few short story incidents demonstrating in particular the Irish humour and way of life. My mother wrote:

On our way to a remote part of the West of Ireland, we sent a telegram to warn the farmer of our arrival, as there was only room for one caravan in the bracken and heather on the edge of a lake. When we arrived there the farmer's sister came running out of the house. By the look on her face it was quite obvious that she had not expected to see us.

"Didn't you get our telegram?" "Telegram? The postman would never deliver me a telegram. He wouldn't want to frighten me!"

Anyway we stayed there some time, and Teddy fished the lake every day. One day when we were in a nearby town having coffee in a café, a man we had never seen before came from another table, sat down at our table and told my husband he had been fishing in the wrong places if he wanted to get fish. He then offered to come over and show us where the salmon lay. He became a good friend and would close his printing business at any time to go fishing with us. One day, he invited us to a garden party at the local lunatic asylum. Why? As he was the printer selected to print the programmes, he was allowed to bring friends!!

Some time later my husband caught a good-sized salmon, which we decided to have smoked. We were told to put it on the train to Galway at 10 o'clock the following morning properly addressed and ticketed. The whole family accompanied the salmon to the station, where the stationmaster said he would show us where to put it when the train came in. About an hour after the scheduled time, the train came in, but every door was locked and no one at that station had a key. So the train moved off on its journey, leaving a dozen passengers and a salmon on the platform to come back the next day.

On another occasion, we were driving along a narrow road when a bus came from the opposite direction. The bus driver was another acquaintance who had gone fishing with us. Just as we were squeezing past each other, he recognised us, stopped the bus and got out, so we stopped as well. He leaned against the door of our car, and told us a long and funny joke. The people in the bus sat waiting and cars began to queue up behind the bus. The driver took his time, no one hooted or seemed at all bothered, and when he finally clambered back into his bus and started to move off, his passengers smiled and waved at us, as did some of the people in the cars behind it.

On our way back across Ireland from Galway, we stopped at a pleasant-looking layby with a grassy verge, and came upon a fascinating sight. A car and caravan were parked at one end of the layby and its occupants had set up a table with a cloth and two chairs outside the van, all nicely laid out for lunch. The lady was putting a salad bowl on the table; the man was sitting on a chair buttering a roll.

At the other end of the layby, perhaps fifty yards away, was a tinker's handcart. A gipsy woman sat on the grass with a bowl on her legs, peeling potatoes. A gipsy man was placing a pot on the fire he had just made. Small children were rolling about or sitting in the dust.

Such a contrast fascinated me.

The next night, we stayed on a site outside Dublin. In the morning, I wanted to telephone to a friend who lived there, and was waiting outside the telephone box at the site when a man with a puzzled expression on his face came out with a small piece of paper in his hand. He turned to me and said, "I don't know what to do with the caravan I hired, and my boat leaves for England in two hours." After questioning him, I found out that he had answered an advertisement and the reply had instructed him to meet the owner and take over the van on a certain street corner, He had duly arrived at the appointed time, and the man and the van were there. He paid for two weeks to the apparent owner, who gave him the piece of paper he was holding, which contained a telephone number. "Ring me when you get back to Dublin and I'll come and fetch it," it said. But the number did not exist, the telephone operator told him, so presumably the "owner" had stolen it and disappeared with two weeks rent!

I often wonder how the man got rid of the van.

*(I don't necessarily disagree with my mother's conclusion, but this is Ireland and my Irish possibilities are: he gave his girl friend's or just another number by mistake, he didn't have the phone with him, etc.).*

Another year, when we stayed at a hill farm in Donegal, friends joined us with their caravan. While our husbands were out fishing, we wives went on long walks. One morning we were out walking when my friend said she had lost a five-pound note (in the 70s in Ireland this was probably enough to keep a couple in food for a week), so we went on the same walk as the previous day to see if she had dropped it. Well we didn't find it, and when we went to the farmhouse for our milk that evening, my friend asked if she could look around the farmyard in case she had dropped it there. There was an old lady sitting by the fire in a rocking-chair and she said she would pray to St. Anthony, the saint who finds lost things, and ask him to find it for her. The next day as my friend was getting some clean towels out of a bed-locker, the five-pound note fell out. Of course she reported it at the farm to the old lady's delight at having her prayers answered.

The next year, we went on our way to the West of Ireland. We found a beautiful place by a loch in Connemara at which to spend a couple of days. We pitched the caravan on a disused road on the very edge of the water, surrounded by blue and purple mountains. We noticed that there was another van further round the lake, and one of the occupants, an Irish lady, came round to see if they could be of help to us. We said everything was fine and invited her to come inside and have coffee with us. This she did, and in the course of conversation, mentioned that her mother had not been out of their van for two days as she had bronchitis. Knowing how far one can be from a chemist in that area, I always took a shelf full of medicines with me, so I asked her if she would like some cough syrup, Vicks or anything else she thought would do her mother good. "Oh, no thank you," she replied, "we're giving her whisky every couple of hours so she won't need anything else."

On arrival at this stretch of coast where we had been before, my husband noticed that one of the caravan tyres was down, so he jacked up the van, took off the wheel and the next day went to the nearest village, which was ten miles away, in the car of my daughter and son-in-law, who were with us with their van and four children. We left the wheel at the garage, told the man where we were staying, which was a mile from the main road on a track across moorland to the sea. He said he would bring it to us that afternoon, about 2 pm which we said would be fine, and we planned to go off for a picnic as soon as it was fixed. In the end, we sent the family off for the picnic, while we continued to wait for our wheel. The Irishman from the garage finally turned up just after 5 pm, jumped out of his car with a jolly greeting... and found he had left our wheel behind at his garage!!!!

I was on some of these holidays with my parents and have some personal anecdotal memories of those times in Ireland. Two of my memories have to do with getting lost in the west because there were lots of lanes and cart-tracks without signposts. We were going along one of these narrow lanes not shown on any map, so not knowing where we were. Suddenly out of the mist trudged an old Irishman carrying a bucket. We stopped him. "We are lost, could you tell us the name of the next town along this road?"

"I could." "Well, what is it?" "'*Tis New York, begorrah!*" And there we were, round the corner from the beach!

On another occasion, we wanted to get to XY town and the road went straight on, but we came to a bridge over a river on our left. We stopped about ten yards short of the bridge and consulted the map: no bridge, no signposts... We saw a man coming from the opposite direction. He leaned against the door and asked, "Can I help you?" "Yes we want to get to XY." "Sure, that's no problem. Ye go shtrait, and ye come to a bridge across a river on your right, so you cross the bridge you turn left and afther 2 miles ye're at XY." My father repeated the instructions to the letter and added that there must be another river. We thanked him, he shrugged his shoulders, said good luck and walked off. A complicated hour later we arrived at XY, and it took some time to unravel where we had gone wrong.

The explanation? The man was facing us when giving directions so he retraced everything in his mind so our left was his right and vice versa!!!!

Many years later, between 2001 and 2005, my mother was invited to the wedding of one of the children of Irish caravanning friends, in the "outback" of the West of Ireland. Fortunately they had arranged a bus for the thirty or forty non-local guests. They made good time and got to know each other, when suddenly the bus stopped. What was the matter? They had come to a fork in the road, and of course no signposts. "No matter," said the driver "With these new mobile telephones I call the office and they'll put us sthraight." According to my mother the conversation went something like this and was on loudspeaker so all could hear:

"I'm lost. I've come to a fork in the road and I don't know which to take."

"Well, where are you exactly?"

"If I knew where I was, I wouldn't be lost, would I? So which fork shall I take?"

"Take the main one."

"They are the same."

"So take the one with the most traffic."

He hung up.

"A lot of use they are..." To cut a longish story short, they arrived an hour-and-a-half late for the church but in time for the wedding feast.

# CHAPTER 12 •
# A Caribbean Holiday

We had met Doug and Alison, but only once (he was a smallish client). Then, one day, out of the blue, we received a letter from them inviting us to spend 12 days with them on their yacht in the Caribbean. The envelope also contained a photo of a beautiful yacht. By chance we had made no special plans that year (1992) so it sounded like a tempting adventure.

Doug, 64, and Alison have been yachting for twenty years. He retired as M.D. of a quoted company where they lived in South Africa at the age of 44, and worked (as a consultant) and sailed alternately until six years ago. He then designed this lovely 52-foot sailing vessel and they (with the help of several paid specialists) spent four years full-time building it in their backyard. They then became full time "yachties," with no fixed residence, a worldwide fraternity that we had never heard of.

We were due to spend overnight in New York on our way to Trinidad where we had a day to spare before meeting up with them. There were already signs of what was to come ( nothing life-threatening but...) in New York. The assistant manager of the hotel forgot to return me my credit card after payment, and then sent it by taxi to 305 West 72 while we were waiting at 305 East 72. Now I really needed Sylvia on the trip as I am unable to forge her signature.

Our programme involved spending our first night at the Holiday Inn in Trinidad, yet there we were in Puerto Rico! What had happened? A world that we didn't know existed. Apparently at the end of the year – at that time anyway – all flights were overbooked and overticketed. Our flight was not the exception, so they had to get people to give up their tickets and take a later plane. We had a big advantage with our spare days before meeting Doug. We discussed giving up ours (Sylvia ultra-reluctant on the re-booking because the desk clerk had said, "Trust me!") and finally gave in to USD 1400.-, a free hotel, three free meals and free transport, if we would spend a night in PR. What a deal! I worked out that on an annual basis for two it came to a million francs a year. I wrote,

"Can one become a professional ticket giver-upper? As I was writing this, Sylvia was scared that we wouldn't get a taxi (it was now Christmas Eve), find that our seats had been double-reserved, and that we would not find our luggage in Trinidad").

We had a nice hotel but... for example when I woke at 8 am and tried to use the phone, they said I couldn't use it because I had checked out an hour earlier! We never found out if I had sleepwalked!

Anyway we had a wonderful day exploring Puerto Rico, a fascinating island with an interesting history, before taking off and going to our rendezvous in Trinidad. We had instructions as to where to meet them but as we got closer and closer it seemed more and more unlikely that we'd find them. Then all of a sudden there was a jetty and there was the yacht!

Our first three days were spent visiting bays close to Port of Spain, then mooring overnight in them. They were close enough to one another that we just used the motor and had no real sailing, but mainly beautiful, spectacular and calm bays. The emptiest had formerly been a leper colony until quite recently. Nowadays none of the lepers visit it because it and the nun's cemetery there are so "spooky". We found it more depressing than anything else; a village of small windowless huts, even when occupied, must have been very primitive, one larger hut where they met and ate together, etc. We took a quick turnaround but the rain and mud – and the rest – chased us away!

Life on board was calm and relaxed, but full of "active inactivity." Doug is a very interesting man with an extremely strong and sometimes aggressive personality. We had discussions on every imaginable subject, and went swimming off the boat or on little empty beaches. But Doug, the ship's captain laid down the rules (the law). "Sylvia, you left the light on: we rely on one solar panel for electricity." "Did you bolt the door?" "Take your shoes off: the sand eats into the wooden deck." "Brush your teeth with the salt water; if it doesn't rain soon, we'll have no fresh water." "I do hope you're enjoying yourself. Life on board is so relaxing.." "Don't hold on to that, it can come away from the wall."...

The first night after the leper colony visit, we dined on board in a lovely little bay before going to bed. "You must leave this porthole open or you won't get enough air in your cabin. The only problem is that in this bay there are vampires, that is vampire bats that get in. They bite and inject an anticoagulant. Our last guest was bitten, lost over a pint-and-a-half of blood and we got him to hospital just in time to stop the bleeding. However you have nothing to worry about because we now know that they keep away from an open flame so we put a candle in the window and that does the trick." Well, you can imagine that neither of us got much sleep, looking at this flickering candle, with the bedcovers drawn tightly up to our noses.

Another bay was occupied by a tribe of howler monkeys, but fortunately we only visited it in the daytime. But the little bays full of the noise of multi-coloured birds and the lush greenery of the coastline made for a most pleasant few days.

One of our few contacts with the outside world was on the third day when a couple of youngsters appeared in our bay offering water-skiing from their boat. Sylvia was an immediate volunteer. But they needed to get more petrol. So we took a few US dollars and went off down the coast with them. The idiots bought oil instead of petrol so we almost ran out on the way back, chug-chugged and finally stopped some 300 yards from the pump and got towed in. After much local-type negotiation, a free-ski promise to a man on shore and the youngster's pawned watch, we finally got our petrol, the trip back to the bay and Sylvia her water-skiing.

Back at port, we took a day off with a local taxi to drive into the hills and visit a nature reserve. Our driver was a typical third-world teenager salesman, who knew it all and had been there before. After one hour into the hills on a twisty winding narrow lane with thick undergrowth on each side, we finally arrived … -at the wrong village. We had to backtrack for one hour into the valley, to take another road back into the hills (by which time the driver admitted that he had never been there before) to an incredibly large manor house built in 1907, where we had a good lunch and then a fascinating walk in the grounds with beautiful old trees and an enormous variety of plants, birds of all shapes, colours and sizes.

On the way back, our third-world driver without a map inevitably took another wrong turn and after a half hour driving through the forest, we found the road blocked by a fifty-foot tree-trunk that had fallen across the road taking all the undergrowth with it. Fortunately, everyone in this country carries a cutlass with them and as the cars started arriving from both directions the drivers all joined in hacking a way through.

Next day was spent on land too but less adventurous, visiting the wonderful old colonial houses of a long ago era and seeing the famous Scarlet Ibis of the Caroni swamps. The next day we were due to do the 77-mile ocean crossing from Trinidad to Grenada, but Alison was unwell so it was postponed for one day and we stayed at anchor completing the preparations.

The ocean crossing under sail was something else. Up at 5 am and at sea by 6: a rough open sea with a 20-knot wind and 15-foot waves, battling against a strong current. 77 miles in ten and a half hours non-stop under 700 square foot of sail is like forever. Sylvia with special anti-sickness patches behind her ears and anywhere else, was fine. I on the other hand with no protection was sick for the first time in 45 years. 7-8 knots is fast, but with the continual pitch and roll, up, up, up aaand doowwn...

Huge ocean waves and beating wind are not the most enjoyable part of sailing...

Grenada (population 110,000), capital St. Georges (pop. 70,000) and a seat at United Nations shouldn't exist but it does. It also has a beautiful coastline and lovely sheltered bays. First night mooring at Prickly Bay with 30 other "yachties," the next day off Hog's Island and on the third we arrived at Secret Harbour where we stayed for the rest of the "holiday." In the meantime we visited St Georges, a lovely little old colonial settlement. In the harbour we saw the eight superb fishing vessels given by Japan to Grenada a year ago. Mutual cooperation? They're still at anchor. No one knows how to operate them.

The "yachties" are an incredible fraternity. Most of them are non-resident anywhere and have been living on their yachts anything from  five to thirty years. They are of all kinds, ages and races but only from developed countries, retired English couples or families, middle-aged Americans, young Dutch families with children born at sea and educated by correspondence courses, boy-friend/girl-friend.

"How many times have you crossed the Atlantic?" "We like this anchorage and may stay here a few months before moving on." We met a French couple in their mid-sixties who had been at it for eight years, spending six months every year at this one anchorage. She painted, he wrote and they didn't even speak English.

## Sylvia's comments

*I enjoyed the holiday even though I felt I was in boarding school. Alison was a wonderful person, a saint, to put up with Doug. ( Do all wives think they're the only ones who say that? He actually wasn't as bad as all that and had plenty of interesting stories to tell).*

*But it was like living on another planet with them. They can spend three months without hearing from or contacting their children, both married in Australia.*

*I found it very difficult to be completely disconnected from the world and unattainable for six days.*

*Maybe I should take some lessons from them!*

*I also thought we were going to sail more, but they hardly ever put up the sails unless travelling to another island between three and ten hours away.*

*Otherwise it is on with the motor and round to the next bay.*

*Back in New York, I had never appreciated a double bed so much and had two hot showers letting the water run for ages. Long live our civilisation*

2913973R00075

Printed in Germany
by Amazon Distribution
GmbH, Leipzig